THE CROSSOVER EXPERIENCE

4

Four Seasons Productions

Four Seasons Productions, LLC.

Copyright © 2022 DJ Kadagian.

A Crossover Experience - Life After Life is Real / DJ Kadagian

ISBN: 978-0-578-94440-1 (Paperback)

ISBN: 979-8-9854846-2-5 (Hardcover)

Book design by Four Seasons Productions

Printed in the United States of America.

First printing edition 2022.

www.4spBooks.com

www.CrossoverExperience.com

THE CROSSOVER EXPERIENCE

LIFE AFTER DEATH IS REAL

What does it look like? What does it feel like?

DJ KADAGIAN

WITH

DR. PIM VAN LOMMEL

GREGORY SHUSHAN, PHD.

4

Forever Sean

CONTENTS

1. INTRODUCTION 1
2. What is a Near-Death Experience? 7
3. Crossover Experience Methodology 13
4. A CROSSOVER EXPERIENCE I 21
5. Your Guides 39
6. Hard Statistics and Nuanced Observations 49
   YOUR JOURNEY BEGINS 63
7. The Out-of-Body Experience 65
8. The Tunnel Experience 85
9. Into the Light(s) 101
10. Deceased Loved Ones & Spiritual Beings 117
11. The NDE Environment 137
12. The Five (+) Senses 157
13. The Life Review 173
14. In the Presence of God 187
15. The Knowledge of Everything 199
16. It is Not Your Time 217
17. The Hellish Realm 233
18. Religion on the Other Side 249
19. How NDEs Change Everyone 265
    A FINAL THOUGHT 285
20. A CROSSOVER EXPERIENCE II 287
    . 305

About the Author 307
Notes 313
Acknowledgments 335

ONE

INTRODUCTION

Life is a dream walking. Death is going home.

Chinese Proverb

What happens when we die? It is one of mankind's most enduring questions. Depictions of an afterlife date back tens of thousands of years. They can be found etched on cave walls and painted on artifacts unearthed at ritual burial sites around the world. It is hidden in sacred burial chambers deep in the Egyptian pyramids, as well as the ancient passage tombs of Scotland and Ireland.

It is depicted in the artwork, places of worship, and sacred texts of the Christians, the Jews, the Muslims, the Hindus, and other religious and spiritual disciplines being practiced around the world today. And yet, it still requires great faith to accept these beliefs — something we find in short supply amidst our fast paced, increasingly materialistic culture.

According to Pew Research, 72% of all Americans and 85% of Christians believe in heaven and an afterlife.[1] However, a much smaller percentage believe in the near-death experience (NDEs). How do we reconcile this? The logical explanation is the former do not believe a person can experience "heaven" and return to tell the tale. And since they have not been there themselves, their belief is a product of faith.

Faith is hard work. And it is often harder to keep. Yet, for those who have had an NDE, faith is no longer necessary — for them, it is fact. They know there is an afterlife because, as they will tell you, they have experienced that realm first-hand.

Many return with stories of meeting a spiritual being — some say they encountered Jesus, some God, and some a pure loving entity. Ninety-six percent tell us that what they experienced was more "real than real."[2] And no one will ever convince them otherwise.

What if the question of the existence of life-after-life could now be answered with certainty? What if we now know what it looks like? What it feels like? Seventy years of research into the near-death phenomenon is providing us this very opportunity.

In the 1960s, stories of people visiting another realm of existence began pouring in from around the world. Medical professionals, particularly cardiologists, at the front line of this new phenomenon began to notice a surge in reports that were closely correlated to recent advances in resuscitation techniques that enabled doctors to bring patients back from clinical death. Something that was not possible before this time.

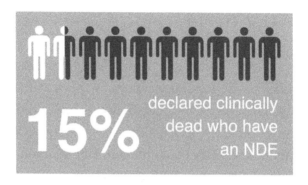

SEE CROSSOVER PROSPECTIVE STUDY COMPILATION - CHAPTER 6

A growing number of researchers affiliated with respected universities and medical institutions the world over began the painstaking process of gathering thousands of testimonials and analyzing what has become known as the near-death experience — a phenomenon that, if proven, would change the way we understand ourselves as a species. Things like why we are here, and what our place is in the universe.

Patterns began to emerge of a remarkably consistent journey of emotional experiences, from the overwhelming love NDErs feel emanating from a brilliant light to the emotional power of a life-review. From the raw sensation of telepathic communication to the collapse of time and space itself. Consistency of experience also extends to the physical environment they encounter — the sweet fragrance of this realm's vibrant gardens, the sound of its otherworldly music, the texture of the mysterious dark tunnel, the visual impact of its gleaming structures.

However, few who have had an NDE have experienced all of its elements. Some will have traveled through the dark tunnel but not walked the gardens. Some will have encountered a being of light but not faced a life-review. And few have experienced the hellish realm. Yet the phenomenon's full wonder — and its implications — present themselves when the full arc of the experience is expressed in one complete journey.

In constructing this book, roughly 200 testimonials were pulled from exceptional NDE experiences out of a pool of over 4,000. Each of these powerful testimonials contains a piece of the NDE journey, with each chapter providing an in-depth look into each of the NDEs major components. Then, as one sprinter passes the baton to the next, we have taken the strongest legs of these collective experiences and connected them together into two powerful journeys for you to experience. From their entry into the tunnel to their return to this realm.

As you are experiencing these journeys, commentary and perspectives are offered by three people who approach them with very different perspectives and skillsets. First, the cardiologist and researcher, who has been "in the trenches" with those experiencing NDEs from the beginning. Then the scholar, who has focused his attention on the current NDE phenomenon through the prism of religion and indigenous cultures throughout human history. And lastly, the quantum economist, whose in-depth experience with statistics and pattern recognition provides both a micro and macro perspective of the data.

Crossover will take you on a wondrous journey through this mysterious, otherworldly realm, in search of a deeper, more expansive understanding of what the NDE is trying to communicate to us.

TWO

What is a Near-Death Experience?

The soul comes from without into the human body, as into a tempo-
rary abode, and it goes out of it anew it passes into other habita-
tions, for the soul is immortal.

RALPH WALDO EMERSON

A near-death experience is a profound and life-changing event that can occur under a number of different circumstances. These include cardiac arrest, which often occurs during a heart attack, shock after hemorrhaging during childbirth, a coma due to traumatic brain injury, or intracerebral hemorrhage and drowning. In this book, we focus exclusively on NDEs that occur during clinical death, which is the closest state to actual death.

In a state of clinical death, most often brought on by cardiac arrest:

• The respiratory center near the brainstem stops functioning, evidenced by the cessation of breathing.

• Blood flow to the brain stops altogether.

• There is a complete loss of electrical activity in the cerebral cortex which results in a flat EEG.

• All brain functioning ceases, and it becomes impossible to be conscious or to form memories.

And yet it is in just this state of clinical death when people are reporting having the most profound experiences of their lives. With survivors reporting these experiences in such high numbers and with such clarity and consistency, they are opening a window into another realm of existence we can no longer ignore.

The Near-Death Experience

Near-death experiences tend to follow a markedly consistent progression beginning with an awareness that the person has died, accompanied by an overwhelming sense of peace.

The majority have an out-of-body experience where, from above, they see their bodies as doctors and nurses attempt to resuscitate them. In a state of enhanced consciousness people describe as more real than real, they find themselves being pulled up and out of the room into what looks like a dark tunnel or path.

They may be met by departed loved ones or spiritual beings who greet them and help guide them forward towards an intense light. As they pass through the tunnel, they enter an expansive world that radiates an unconditional love they cannot fully articulate.

All around them they describe a wondrous beauty. Colors they have never experienced before. Flowers and grass and trees that glow with energy. Light coming, not from the sun, but radiating from everything within this realm. Time loses all meaning as past, present, and future melds into one.

They may meet a spiritual being who will guide them on a life-review. Here they will see and relive all the events of their lives. But this time, they will also experience them from the perspective of those who were affected by those events — good and bad.

Some will describe meeting God or a god-like figure radiating an intense and absolute love. They are in awe and humbled that they would be the subject of this being's complete and absolute attention. They express feelings as if they are finally home.

They may have questions answered, discover their life's purpose, receive insights into the meaning of our existence. Some will be shown the mysteries of the universe itself.

Some say they felt they were there for hours. For others, it felt like days or even months. But ultimately a border is reached. Some are given a choice to stay, but most are told their work is not finished, and they must go back.

None want to re-enter their bodies — not just for the physical pain. They experienced so much more freedom in what felt like their truer manifestation. They do not see how they will fit into a physical body that now seems so small and confining.

And upon their return, they describe an intense sadness at having to leave this realm, but a comfort in knowing they will, one day, return.

So, are these NDEs real?

The statistical significance of the vast amount of peer reviewed, published research accumulated by independent researchers and those associated with respected universities and medical institutions around the world, can no longer be ignored. Nor can it be explained away as mere chance.

NDE reports worldwide are striking in their similarity, regardless of a person's culture, race, gender, sexuality, or religious beliefs. Another commonality is the permanent shift in attitudes and beliefs that follow an NDE. Changes that do not occur with those having reported clinical death who did not also experience an NDE.

Most express being more accepting of others and much less tied to the material world, with 75% transitioning into new careers[1] and 54% reporting major life changes with follow-up studies 20 years later showing virtually no falloff in the intensity they originally experienced.[2]

Further strengthening the data's veracity is corroboration from doctors and nurses of what survivors describe happening in the operating room during clinical death — the most irrefutable proof of an NDE. Crossover's compilation of prospective and retrospective studies report out-of-body experiences with a range of 37% and 65%[3] respectively, in which NDErs can accurately recount what was said and done during resuscitation, from a vantage point outside their bodies.

This phenomenon also supports the theory of non-local consciousness — a consciousness beyond and apart from our physical bodies. With our growing understanding of quantum physics, much of this data is being revealed as having a basis in science as well.

It has become clear that we are much more than the physical, material world we see around us. We are much more than our bodies. Death is not an end to our being; it is merely a transition into a different, more expansive existence. It is no longer necessary to debate the existence of an afterlife. It is time we now begin to embrace and discuss its implications for each of us, and the human race itself.

THREE

Crossover Experience Methodology

The day science begins to study non-physical phenomena, it will make more progress in one decade than in all the previous centuries of its existence.

NICOLA TESLA

There are five main sources of information and content about the near-death experience:

1. Written testimonials gathered in a systematic and structured format, which can be found online at a handful of websites that focus on the near-death experience. The most important of these is the Near-Death Experience Research Foundation (NDERF.org) founded and maintained by Jeffery and Joy Long. This is by far the largest repository of testimonials, which number over 5,000 and have been gathered over more than 20 years.

2. YouTube, where you will find interviews, lectures, and panel discussions hosted by NDE organizations such as the International Association for Near-Death Studies (IANDS.org), as well as respected universities and medical conferences, religious organizations, and platforms such as Ted Talks.

3. Books, which range from personal NDE encounters to the most up-to-date research and science on the subject.

4. Peer-reviewed prospective and retrospective studies and research published with reputable organizations.

5. Documentary films, which are more limited in number and scope.

The most valuable source of content, of course, comes directly from the source itself. A near-death experience, when articulated by someone who has crossed over, is nothing if not experiential. And the experiential will be the closest we can come to understanding the wonder and power of these journeys.

Fortunately, you cannot help but be pulled into these truly remarkable stories. Why? It is the near-death experiencer's absolute certainty that what they experienced was "more real than real" that will leave a lasting impression on you. You will see it in the expression on their face, hear it in the inflection in their voice, and be struck by the consistency of their experiences across race, gender, religious belief, and culture. And you will come to understand and appreciate the underlying purpose of them sharing their very personal story.

Over time, you may find that written testimonials have the most impact on you — and this is the primary source we pull from in this book. This is, in large part, due to the inherently different form and style in the way we tend to articulate ourselves between oral and written form. One of the differences between writing and speaking styles is the use of complex sentences.

In writing, complex sentences are necessary for adding the right level of detail and precision, and these complex sentences can be made easier to digest and assimilate with the right punctuation. Conversely, complex sentences are deadly in oral presentations. They flatten out delivery and risk losing the audience in the experiential component.

Writing and speaking also differ in the degree and importance of word choice. In writing, you want to choose your words very carefully. A well-chosen word can often make or break the point you are making. In speaking, the exact words you choose are not as important as the general point you are trying to convey. Just as you remember the general arc of a play, not the specific lines, your audience will remember your ideas, not your specific words. You may find that once you have experienced the broader strokes painted in the testimonials you experience in oral form, you will want to drill down into the more focused and finer details being conveyed in written form.

We will provide comments at the end of each chapter, which include a range of possibilities. What you see in your mind's eye or experience in your heart may differ markedly from our interpretations, yet be more relevant to you. For those who want "just the facts," and to experience these journeys unfiltered, we recommend you skip over the comment sections.

The testimonials contained in this book were curated from a pool of over 4,000 near-death experiences. In addition to these being exceptional testimonials with a high degree of detail, there are a number of screeners applied in assembling this collection for you. Some may find these screeners to be too limiting. While it is not the intent to minimize the validity of any NDE, statistical analysis plays a very big role in the content of this book, and we tried to provide the most irrefutable, accurate, and descriptive NDEs possible:

1. The NDE must have occurred during clinical death — the closest state to actual death, which will be described in greater detail in the following chapter. Clinical death must have occurred in a hospital setting or in the presence of an EMT or trained medical professional in the field (there are a handful of exceptions in a pool of hundreds).

2. Testimonials must be first-person accounts. An NDE is often difficult for the experiencer to articulate — there is a "you had to be there" quality to the experience. It is possible that the fine, yet important details, are lost in translation.

3. For similar reasons, all testimonials are chosen from those 14 years or older. It is possible that the average 13-year-old will have a more limited vocabulary and difficult time articulating their experience. They may also have had to work through their understanding of their experience with a parent or other adult. Translating their experiences might be altered by this dynamic.

4. The person must have had only one near-death experience in their lifetime, unless they experienced clinical death more than once during the same medical episode.

5. Their experience must fall within the framework of what is generally understood to occur during an NDE. For example, no one would be included in this book who met with aliens during their NDE.

Crossover endeavors to highlight NDEs that you would only have come across had you been fortunate to spend time on a website such as NDERF, which utilizes a very structured questionnaire that a near-death experiencer must fill out. This format provides a more uniform and detailed description of a near-death experience. Additionally, since these testimonials are given anonymously and are not promoted, it is less likely that they are embellished, or that certain features are emphasized or de-emphasized to speak to a particular audience.

All testimonials are laid out word for word as they were told. We have added some punctuation and corrected for spelling when necessary. While, in some cases, the sequence of a sentence within a paragraph may have been altered for clarity, nothing has been taken out of context and no language has been added or removed.

Here are several other factors that are important to consider:

• The purpose of this book is not to convince you of whether NDEs are real. This is a conclusion you must come to on your own.

• ***This is not a book full of statistics***, although you will find distilled, relevant data throughout. A treasure-trove of NDE research can be found on our website at www.CrossoverExperience.com. There, you will have access to the most important, peer-reviewed NDE studies in down-loadable format, as well as links to books and websites dedicated to the subject. You will also find our carefully curated collection of NDE testimonials, interviews and lectures.

• The three contributors to this book believe that near-death experiences are real. Two believe that they are proof of an afterlife, while one is agnostic in this regard.

• Two contributors to this book have a belief in God while one is agnostic.

• We do not describe the circumstances that lead to a person experiencing an NDE. Since all near-death experiences in this book occur during clinical death, the focus is on the experience itself.

Crossover Experience is, as its name implies, an opportunity for you to experience, in greater depth, what this otherworldly realm looks like, sounds like, and feels like.

No matter where you find yourself at the end of your journey here — from NDE believer, to interested observer, or open-minded skeptic — we recommend you continue searching out and working through the massive reservoir of information about the NDE that has been accumulated over the past five decades.

As for the structure of this book — in short order, we will be introducing you to three people from very different personal and professional backgrounds who will be going on this journey into the otherworldly realm of the NDE with you. This will be followed by a look at the commonalities and differences between near-death experiences that become apparent in researching thousands of NDEs. This should help orient you for our entry into a more in-depth look at each stage of the NDE.

Finally, we will finish this journey the way we are about to start it — on a full NDE narrative. Built from 40 different testimonials, these stories present the full arc of an NDE if it included all of the common experiences, in linear form. This is an extremely rare occurrence. However, each of the stages covered, in themselves, have been experienced millions of times worldwide.

Ours is one such story — a possibility.

FOUR

A CROSSOVER EXPERIENCE I

"I AM FINALLY HOME"

Death is not extinguishing the light; it is putting out the lamp because dawn has come.

RABINDRANATH TAGORE

I can remember thinking, this is weird, I'm hearing far off and faint voices, but aren't I being operated on? These voices weren't anything I could discern. They were just far off - distant. I could hear them, but I wasn't making anything out of what was being said.

As time passed, it seemed as if those far off voices were coming somehow closer to me. They were beginning to be more and more distinct. And as they came closer, I began to think I wonder what they're saying? So I began paying closer attention to them.

Again, as time passed, I could now hear what was being

said. Although the voices were still somewhat distant, there was this feeling of clarity in what was being said. As I began to understand, they were reciting vital signs. Nothing terribly exciting, just blood pressure: so and so, respiration: so and so, heart beat: so and so.

I remember thinking, 'I'll be damned, they're talking about someone being operated on.' And at the same moment, realizing that I was being operated on - 'isn't that a coincidence?' All the while, as these voices were becoming more and more clear, it dawned on me that the vital signs they were reciting were deteriorating proportionately to the clarity of my hearing what was happening.....my heart stopped while I was being operated on.

All at once, I heard one of the nurses yell out, "Straight line, straight line, my God! We've got a straight line!" [1]

It was at that moment in time I had a brief pause in my thoughts away from the passing events and then I realized very clearly, I had died.

No event in my life has ever been so clear to me. This experience was exact, with meaning and purpose. This was natural order. My body had or was well in the process of dying.

No events in my awakening state of mind have ever reached this level of conscious awareness. I briefly remembered the emergency room and that something had gone wrong but it did not matter. It was the most profound moment of my life. Very emotional for me to admit. I was not of my body any longer. I was of my soul. [2]

I became aware of 'everything', such as my position on the table and the movement of the earth. It wasn't quite like I was dissolving, but rather like I was disconnecting or becoming unsynchronized with the universe. I was calmly aware of everyone around me and what they were doing. I know I was not connected to my body.

I was on my way to somewhere else, but there are no words to describe it. Words like 'up' or 'down' lacked meaning. It was that disconnected experience, as though the connected portion of our existence blocks another realm, whatever that is. I just know I was on my way to the next realm. I was not frightened but very accepting of it because this was just a transition.[3]

Then, the room folded in from the ceiling and I started rising, each time faster and higher. I started to feel an extraordinary liberation of my soul from my body. It was as if I had been released from a lifetime sentence; as if my body had been my jail (without being conscious of this until now). Everything that connected me to it was heavy and burdensome: having to breathe, having to move my body, etc., as if the bonds from childhood carried family, friends, acquaintances, the town, etc.[4]

One of my first revelations was that I was still 'ME'. The importance of this is difficult to explain but it was a surprise to me and a deep joy. I was not a mistake and I was who I was always meant to be. I vaguely remember moving to places and the realization that although I was still me, I now moved through barriers without restriction.[5]

I went through the wall where it joined the ceiling. I wasn't outside in the cold or ending up on another floor of the hospital after going through the wall. A tunnel enveloped me and kept swiftly going backwards. But I had no sense of motion.[6]

At first, I found myself in absolute darkness, but was totally aware of everything and knew that I was dead. There was no fear or anxiety attached to this awareness. In fact I knew that I was 'in death' (the darkness had a presence to it).

I remember turning to my left, right, and thinking, 'now what?' There was no point to moving anywhere. I had no reference point, nothing. Nihilism, the ultimate individualism, just myself in a void of emptiness. God had left me there just long enough to become familiar with this reality. I then found myself being lead along, but I wasn't moving by my own ability. It was more like being carried along. I felt as if there was a hand on my back directing me, or more like being placed in God's hand and transported along without my effort. I had the awareness of movement, but no reference of moving because I was in complete darkness.[7]

I became aware of the darkness getting lighter and lighter, and then eventually going to a medium shade of gray. Then I became aware that I was floating upward through this grayness. Then I broke through and rose up into this flat plain, with almost like an indistinct mistiness for 'ground.' I immediately saw this wall of gray stone blocks on my left. They didn't seem very tall. Although I don't have anything for reference, I'd say 20 feet tall. They were large blocks, rough on the surface, and dark gray (like wet stone blocks) that seemed to stretch all the way out to infinity.

I was also acutely aware that I had no body. I was facing the wall at like a 30 or 45 degree angle, not looking straight at it, but I could see that it had no end. My eye could follow it as it stretched out to the horizon and beyond. Close by, there was a doorway in the wall. The door was open with the hinge on the right side and opening outwards. Due to the angle, I couldn't see what was on the other side of the door.

Coming out of this doorway were whitish, pearlescent, tendrils of light, which were flowing out and dissipating. I was overcome with an emotional blend of relief, love, and acceptance. I was 'coming home' and that everything was going to be alright.[8]

This is where it gets very difficult to describe what I happened, because I can't find words that fit the experience. I saw a light that defies description. It was so beautiful and seemed to be in complete harmony with sound and other sensory input that also defy description. It was not of this world.[9]

When I emerged on the other side of the light, it reminded me of a warm summer day that was very sunny; after a day where the colors of the sky, earth, trees, and flowers were very vivid. They were radiating with the moisture that came off the ground, only more vividly than I ever remembered before. It was an open field with flowers as bright as poppies where everything was painted because all was so vivid.[10]

A little ways away from me were three horses who were pasturing. In life, I had never seen horses like these. The size was something between a pony and a race horse, even though by appearance I know horses a bit; however, no such heavenly horses like that had I ever seen. About ten years after this experience, I was in Iceland and I saw something that shocked me because the Icelandic horses were like the heavenly horses in every detail.[11]

It was really beautiful, with gardens and fountains and small, countryside hills. The people appeared in Greek or Roman dress, very comfortable with white robes and sandal type shoes. A pocket of females was conversing near a majestic water fountain that also displayed Greek decor, with Seraphim, ivy and fruit. I didn't know what to do or say, so I just stood there and looked at them.[12]

I felt content and loved, but this feeling was not separate from the light, sound, or floating. Everything was all one experience. That's why I have a hard time describing what was going on. Nothing was separate from anything else. Then I heard encouraging voices behind my head saying so gently and lovingly 'Come on; it's okay.'[13]

Everything had an extra dimension to things. Everything looked more real. I remember taking note of how people looked. The only explanation that I have is that I was able to see roundly. When we see people normally, we only get to see what they want to reveal. This was like seeing people for who they are, as God sees them: all at once. Also, the white gowns were part of people; it wasn't like they had put clothing on as a separate fabric, but that it was an extension of who they were, like the robe of salvation, or the gown of righteousness, from scripture. They all looked young, but were not young in age. They were just freed from the decay and curse of death. They were fully alive.[14]

There were others that appeared human, and others that were human like, and still others that were light beings. The ones I felt were angelic were the tall ones with longhair; I could not tell if they were male or female, maybe neither. The light beings were brilliant rainbows, I felt very joyful in their presence, and then there were the human ones, but were very bright like the light itself.[15]

I have a vague recollection of having my Earthly experiences 'downloaded', and having a great reunion with these beings, with a great period of relaxation/recuperation. Communication was non-verbal and instantaneous. It involved relaying entire occurrences, concepts, and events with associated emotions, not just words and sentences.[16]

These people started guiding me down this pathway...and this pathway was the most beautiful experience I could ever imagine. The thing that absolutely speaks to my soul moves me to tears is color. The intensities of colors. The intricacies of Flowers. The aromas of flowers that to me speaks beauty. And that is what I experienced.

This pathway was not only woven together with fibers of God's love but exploded with every color of the universe and some that don't exist here. And flowers - there were too many to count. And these beautiful aromas - I was experiencing them all at once. There again there was a shift in time so that I could see it and understand the colors and hear the colors. I know that doesn't make sense, but that's what it was like.[17]

I remember there was a bright mist permeating everything. The light was everywhere; it even passed through me!...Everything had an overall whiteness and brightness about it. You could see the color bright green of the plants. I could see the water and a bright glow surrounded everything.

The water was so sparkling clean. I remember wanting to bend over and take a drink from the stream that was running through this garden we were walking through. When I tried to scoop up the water in my hands the water ran through my hands, literally, and it wasn't wet.... My thirst for this water, even though I wasn't able to put it to my lips and drink it, was gone.

I can't describe the sensation I felt when the water was passing through my hands but I did feel something, though. I felt this overwhelming desire to experience everything about this garden.[18]

I was then aware of being whisked away in the arms of a being I could not see. I knew I was being carried by a being and that this being had no physical body nor did I. Below, I saw a beautiful island-like city that was glowing with vivid color. There was no sun in the sky; the island city just glowed all on its own.[19]

I saw a city of large buildings in the distance. The buildings were the color of gold and my guide told me they were gold. My guide told me if I wished I could think of being closer to the city and I would be. Sure enough, I thought of being closer, and suddenly I was at the very edge of the golden city. I saw little water falls in the flower gardens that were absolutely breathtaking. I felt so good.[20]

Then I found myself walking on a very smooth path that was about twenty feet wide, following the sound of music and angels singing. It was beautiful! I went through very large gates that were made of iron and gold, with small golden figures attached to them. I saw a wall that was made of cut stone. It was very smooth to the touch.[21]

I felt myself to be very awake and aware the whole time. I was immensely curious and observing, and my awareness was unearthly, much larger than when I am here in life. I could see 360 degrees around myself. I could focus on what I wanted to and keep it close-up without any problems, even without thinking about it. I could look up, down, forward and behind me all at once.

I felt more fresh and energized than ever, much more than when I am in life. I had the feeling that I could do anything, not that I thought about it, but I had no problems at all, and never speculated on anything negative. I was energized, joyful and curious. I was there in the present moment, totally in the present...with all the emotions and experiences, together with this vibrant and very loving being who I just knew so well, without knowing from where, other than it must have been when I was in the afterlife, when I have been physically dead.[22]

I began to see events appearing along the surface of a million large screen TV's, or panels lining the walls but that is poor description as to what I really experienced. The events seemed to surround me from all sides. I felt at first without realization, some connection to these events. Within a few seconds, I realized it was my life, memories, and events that only I would understand and put meaning to.

The color and clarity where exactly as I had remembered them. These memories and events where passing through my mind with incredible visual perspective, each was alive and in absolute detail and I could touch and feel them all at the same time.[23]

I saw myself doing everything and anything that I had ever done in my entire life. I saw who I was. What I was doing, whatever it was, with and in addition to watching this pass before my eyes. I felt all feelings. Not only my own. But I felt the feelings of those that I was with when any event happened. Nothing told me what I did was either right or wrong. I just inherently knew and understood the good and the bad. But no one was pointing a finger of accusation at me for anything that I had ever done.[24]

Then of in the distance out of the blackness to my right I see a man and he slid up right up to my face...just boom, he's in my face. He didn't walk bouncy he slid. He was the most beautiful being I ever saw.

I was enveloped in pure love, a feeling that I cannot describe - pure love and peace and wellbeing, safety. A glowing love like no other that I can't describe how wonderful it was. He was the big cheese. That is what I call him now. It was GOD. There is a GOD. a supreme being, the one.

He had long white hair past his shoulders wavy the color of that fiberglass stuff in furnace filters. It looked softer than anything I ever saw he had a beard long wavy soft white... His skin was a golden bronze color almost metal like. Polished old brass he was a perfect being, he was so pretty. He was the most beautiful thing I ever saw.

He was wearing a kaftan with bell sleeves and gold embroidery around the collar sleeves and hem with a Nuru collar. I sew. It was like a rayon thin silky flowing, you could tell he was buff under it. I was in pure love. His eyes were not of a color that is here on earth. The color was not in our human rainbow.

When I looked into his eyes all the secrets of the universe were revealed to me. The universe was created right in front of my eyes. I saw everything that has ever happened since the beginning of the Big Bang. Like the Discovery Channel. I saw everything, the whole universe from the beginning of time.[25]

I was allowed to have full knowledge and understanding. I remember that the awareness hit me with complete clarity and I thought, 'Of course, it's so obvious. Why are we all missing it?' Although not allowed to keep all the knowledge shown to me, there are two items I was allowed to keep: 1) In response to my question regarding religions of the world and which is the 'true' religion, HE answered 'Men come to me on many paths,' and I had the complete understanding of the response, which is broader than the words can convey. The point is not religion, but faith.

In response to my question about why we are here, HE answered 'To love one another.' Again, the understanding and meaning of HIS answer is so much more than the words. We are each part of HIM and by loving one another (and ourselves), we are in fact loving HIM.[26]

Then I was told that I had to go back, which didn't make me happy at all, as I knew that being alive would hurt.

Every aspect of living would hurt. The thought of going back into a wet, disgusting body repulsed me. I couldn't believe I had to wear my body again, as it felt like wearing an old disgusting coat that belonged to someone else. Finally I was told that this was my last chance and that I should have the courage to live the life I wanted to live.[27]

Suddenly something caught the back of my body and I was pulled rapidly backwards and back through the tunnel. Everything became very cold as soon as the light went out.[28]

I began to go back down the tunnel in reverse. On the way, much was being erased from my memory. Not the event itself, but the newfound universal knowledge, the details.I felt sucked into my body and woke up and the air was heavy, movement more difficult, even moving an arm, not from any physical inability but this is the way earth is, very primordial compared to where I just was. I recall asking if I was in heaven. The doctor was frightened, upset, and said they nearly lost me.[29]

I recall starting to cry and asking them 'why did you bring me back to this place. It was so nice there. Everyone was so nice and loved each other. It was so beautiful. Why did you have to bring me back here?' Those nearby seemed to hear me and seemed shocked, but remained professional, as I recall.

I was quiet for a while processing what I remembered of the experience while they worked. I recall eventually asking them not to tell my husband that I didn't want to come back. I'm quite sure they thought I was an ungrateful lunatic, but they were relieved I was alive.[30]

I still knew some things and when alone with my husband I told him to listen carefully and remember what I was telling him because it was being erased. And as quickly as I was telling him things, it was being erased just as quickly. When I finished I asked him if he got all I told him. He looked at me strangely. I asked again. Then he told me that I sounded like I was speaking a foreign language and he could not understand anything I said to him previously. He was alarmed. By then, all of the universal knowledge was gone. But not the *experience*.[31]

I can't believe what I have lived, felt, and the worst thing - now I know it. You must live until you don't know when, but with the happiness at the same time of knowing that I will return and that they await me and I will do everything possible for that to be the case. And it is so easy and it is so easy and simple.[32]

I learned, after the NDE, that I have a choice all the time as to how I want to structure my experience, and I can follow any path I want. It doesn't matter once we cross over to the other side. It simply does not count for ANYTHING.... ever. So why choose a harsh life experience? We don't have too...We use far too much energy trying to live our earthly lives in a way we believe constitutes happiness; but it is such an illusion. I experienced the ease of living without money, status, time, etc.[33]

I saw many, many things, and many things made sense to me then. I felt I had a twofold purpose: one, to live in a new, courageous way, honoring my relationships and living a deeper life; two, I had a conviction that I had a special work to do, which involved educating people or doing research about life after death, consciousness or whatever! I wanted to tell the world about what I had found, learned and discovered.

I felt an unshakable sense that mankind's theories about life and death were wrong, that the truth is so much bigger so as to escape logic. It's the relationships that can transform any of us. Even though I have been a therapist for twenty-nine years, I didn't see the shimmering significance, beauty and power of our relationships. Now I give much more to my relationships. I still make mistakes, but I correct them and move on. There is no point in arguing and fighting. We are all the same. We are in essence one.

I doubt I'll ever shake the deep-seated conviction that all earthly philosophical and ontological belief systems are simply misguided. It's just not the way people think, theorize or imagine it to be 'over there'. People are meaning makers, so it's understandable how thousands of different ideas have emerged over the millennia. There may be elements of truth in all or many of them. But I NOW believe the big picture cannot be grasped, except as through a NDE or some unusual mystical experience or extra-ordinary phenomenon. And even then, it can only be surmised or grasped in part.[34]

I believed in some kind of spirituality before the event. After, I believe that all is spirit, and there is no doctrine that contains all the essence of the spirit that comprises our lives. There is no meaning for me in studying religion because, I know for certain, it is a human construction. I still long, for a stronger connection to the vastness of the spirit of all things.[35]

I honestly don't care what other people think about my experience. It was MY experience. To me, it's truth. To me, nothing was linear and it all existed outside of time. That experience was more real to me than what anyone said was happening in the hospital. It brings me peace, and raises so many questions. I have experienced a moment of enlightenment and walked in death.[36]

I now know that there is a life after death. I now know that there is no hell other than the one we create ourselves. I know the most important thing is love between people and all beings. I know that we are here to learn and reflect in each other. I know that I receive as much help from the other side, as I am ready to receive, from those who I am most connected to in love.

I now know that those who are passed away sometimes visit me and follow what happens in my life.

I now know that I have set myself for something good, that I will reach in this life.

I now know that all my children have chosen me as a mother, in love.

I now know that I am loved.

I now know that I am here in this life to, among other things, learn to love myself.

I now know that there is a *meaning* with it all - why we are here.[37]

FIVE

Your Guides

RESEARCHER - SCHOLAR - QUANTUM ECONOMIST

The boundaries between life and death are at best shadowy and vague. Who shall say where one ends and where the other begins?"

Edgar Allen Poe

DJ Kadagian

My initial interest in the near-death experience began 25 years ago when I came across Raymond Moody's groundbreaking book Life After Life, which was originally published in 1975. I spent time familiarizing myself with the subject, while I was studying the subject of death — from the Tibetan Book of the Dead to the psychedelic experience, and most everything in between. However, I ran into two roadblocks that kept me from digging further into the NDE. One was not being able to find enough fact-driven data that could satisfy the skeptic in me. The second roadblock was a lack of faith that I could overcome the thought, "If something appears to be too good to be true, it usually is."

As someone who operates in the world of quantum economics, developing computer-based trading programs, I am forever monitoring the financial markets and looking for patterns — or a "wrinkle" — that others do not see which may give me an advantage over my competition. I cannot afford to rely on faith. And fact, as I have come to learn, is in the eye of the beholder. Thirty years engaged in this work has tuned me to recognize anomalies anywhere. Some are interesting, some are useful, and some are truly profound. With the vast amount of data and testimonials now available to analyze, I have come to believe that the NDE is the mother of all wrinkles in a universe teeming with them.

I am certainly not the only person who has recognized this. Even despite not experiencing an NDE myself. Yet as a highly trained skeptic with a knack for identifying those wrinkles, crunching vast amounts of data in unorthodox ways and connecting the many dots that reveal themselves, I believe my-arm's length approach to the NDE has been an advantage. It has enabled me to take a dispassionate and unbiased approach in focusing my very particular skill set on the phenomena — analyzing the research, gaining a cursory understanding of the relevant quantum science and, most importantly, immersing myself in thousands of testimonials searching for subtle patterns that might yield more insight into the NDE.

This process has enabled the skeptic in me to sift out a micro and macro roadmap that has led to a conclusion I have a high degree of confidence in. And it has taught me that fact and faith are not mutually exclusive — a quality particularly relevant to the near-death phenomenon which has a mountain of subjective, objective, and retrospective evidence. Once measured, it is hard to argue with, and harder still to ignore. This characteristic is further strengthened by the fact that no skeptic of the NDE, in my research, has advanced any large sample size, statistically significant studies of their own in the 50 years it has been studied. Certainly none that are peer reviewed. And most revealing — none of these skeptics have experienced an NDE themselves.

So much evidence is pointing to the existence of life after death. If it truly does exist, it is the biggest story, by an order of magnitude, of any in human history. How could I not — how could we not — explore this phenomenon more deeply?

Dr. Pim van Lommel

In 1969, during my rotating internship, a patient was successfully resuscitated in the coronary care unit by electrical defibrillation. We mostly do not realize anymore that about 50 years ago, all patients with cardiac arrest died because modern resuscitation techniques like defibrillation and external chest compression were not yet available. So before those years nobody survived a cardiac arrest. But this patient regained consciousness after a period of unconsciousness of about 4 minutes, and we as the resuscitation team were of course incredibly happy. But the patient seemed to be extremely disappointed. He told me about going through a tunnel, seeing a light and beautiful color, and hearing music.

I have never forgotten this event, but I did not do anything with it. And in that time I did not know that in human history the same experiences have been told, in many cultures, in many religions and in all times. Only years later, in 1975, Raymond Moody first described the so-called "near-death experiences". I first read about these experiences in the book by George Ritchie entitled "Return from Tomorrow," which relates what he experienced during a period of clinical death of 9-minutes duration in 1943 during his medical study. After reading this book, I started to interview my patients who had survived a cardiac arrest. And to my great surprise, within two years, 12 patients out of 50 survivors of cardiac arrest in the past told me about their NDE.

So for me, it all started with scientific curiosity, because according to our current medical concepts, it is not possible to experience consciousness during a cardiac arrest, when circulation and breathing have ceased! I grew up in an academic environment, in which I had been taught that it was obvious that consciousness was the product of a functioning brain. And up until that point, I had always accepted this as indisputably true. But now the phenomenon of near-death experience raised several fundamental questions: viii / How and why does an NDE occur? How does the content of an NDE come about? Why does an indie bring about such profound changes in someone's life? I was unable to accept some of the answers to these questions because they seemed incomplete, incorrect, or unsubstantiated.

Science means asking questions with an open mind. Science should be the search for explaining new mysteries, rather than sticking with old concepts. He who has never changed his mind because he could not accept new concepts has rarely learned something. We desperately need a real paradigm shift in science to understand consciousness and its relation with brain function, and I sincerely hope that quantum physicist Max Planck was wrong when he said in 1934: 'A new scientific truth does not triumph by convincing its opponents and making them see the light, but rather because its opponents eventually die, and a new generation grows up that is familiar with it' (Planck, 1948, pp. 33–4).

Current science must reconsider its hypotheses about the nature of perceptible reality, because these ideas have led to the neglect or denial of significant areas of conscious-ness. Current science usually starts from a reality based solely on objective, physical phenomena. It detests subjec-tivity and enshrines objectivity, because it wants to depend on objective data rather than on subjective experiences. Yet at the same time one can (intuitively) sense that besides objective, sensory perception there is a role for subjective aspects such as feelings, inspiration, and intuition. As stated before, current scientific techniques are incapable of measuring or demonstrating the content of thoughts, feel-ings, and emotions. A purely materialist analysis of a living being cannot reveal the content and nature of our consciousness.

It often takes an NDE to get people to think about the

possibility of experiencing consciousness independently of the body and to realize, that presumably, consciousness always has been and always will be, that everything and everybody is connected, that all of our thoughts will exist forever, and that death as such does not exist. But also, the results and conclusions of scientific studies on NDE provide an opportunity to reconsider our relationship with ourselves, our fellow man, and nature, but only if we are willing and able to ask open questions and abandon preconceptions. Studies into NDE may help the scientific community to reconsider some assumptions about life and death, and about consciousness and its relationship with brain function.

Gregory Shushan, Phd.

I first read about near-death experiences as an adolescent, in books that collected accounts of unexplained phenomena – showers of frogs and fishes, UFO sightings, bigfoot, stigmata, lucid dreams, precognition, and so on. The sections on ghosts, mediumship, and reincarnation particularly stood out to me, although not as much as the ones on NDEs.

Later I stumbled on Carol Zaleski's Otherworld Journeys: Accounts of Near-Death Experience in Medieval and Modern Times (Oxford University Press, 1987). The book is a comparison between modern accounts of NDEs and medieval European visionary texts about monks traveling to afterlife realms and coming back. So I went straight from childhood sensationalist reading about NDEs to a scholarly study of historical NDEs, bypassing Moody and other early near-death studies altogether. My reading on the subject remained casual at that point, but the phenomenon, and especially the fact that it was known from other times in history, stayed with me and evidently started taking root.

Fast-forward to my studies for a degree in Egyptology at University College London's Institute of Archaeology. I was reading Egyptian afterlife texts – the Book of the Dead, Coffin Texts, Pyramid Texts, and so on – and some of the general themes were very familiar from what I'd read about NDEs. I started wondering: Could the similarities between these afterlife beliefs and NDEs mean that ancient Egyptians were having these experiences themselves and even basing their religion upon them?

Given the similarities between NDEs, European medieval afterlife texts, and ancient Egyptian afterlife texts, I wondered how far this correlation could extend. So for my MA thesis, I compared ancient Egyptian and ancient Vedic Indian afterlife beliefs in relation to NDEs. The project snowballed and for my PhD in Religious Studies at University of Wales Lampeter, I expanded it to include ancient China, Sumerian and Old Babylonian Mesopotamia, and Aztec and Maya Mesoamerica.

To be clear, for the most part, the texts I looked at were not historical descriptions of the NDEs of actual individuals. While there were odd examples here and there, as well as some clear references to the phenomenon, most of the material I looked at in these ancient civilizations concerned religious beliefs in an afterlife. Essentially, I was trying to establish which of these civilizations had beliefs that were congruent with NDEs. And what I found was that a consistent set of thematic similarities corresponded to nine of the most common elements of NDEs. These included out-of-body experiences, seeing one's own "corpse," entering darkness, going to other realms, encountering deceased relatives, beings of light, life review, barriers or obstacles, and transcendence or becoming god-like.

The implication was clear: The very existence of the cross-cultural similarities indicated that experience preceded conception – that is, near-death experiences contributed to the formation of afterlife beliefs in all these largely independent, unconnected ancient civilizations. To argue the reverse would not explain how this set of thematically similar ideas could be independently invented, or why they would bear such similarities to NDEs. This study became the basis for my first book, Conceptions of the Afterlife in Early Civilizations (Bloomsbury, 2009).

These conclusions are not meant to ignore the differences. They are just as prominent and just as important as the similarities. NDEs don't occur in an identity-less vacuum, and cultural conditioning does not disappear simply because one is in an altered state of consciousness. The problem of differences became the subject of my next study, albeit inadvertently. With a fellowship at the Ian Ramsey Centre for Science and Religion, and funding from the Perrott-Warrick Fund at Trinity College Cambridge, I undertook a comparison of NDEs and afterlife beliefs in the indigenous societies of Africa, Oceania, and North America. My sources this time were the accounts of Western explorers, missionaries, and anthropologists, from the 16th to early 20th centuries. Given the clear results of my previous study, I fully expected this one to replicate it. This was not to be the case, however.

I unearthed over 70 Native American NDEs or references to them, along with more than 20 statements that their afterlife beliefs were based directly on such experiences. Similarly, from Polynesia and Melanesia I found 36 NDEs alongside 19 statements that they were the source of afterlife beliefs. This contrasts sharply to Micronesia, Australia, and Africa where very few NDEs were reported. In societies in those regions, there was less interest in speculations about afterlives in otherworlds, and more of a focus on the activities of ancestor spirits remaining on Earth. It's not that individuals in these societies didn't have NDEs – it's that they didn't valorize them or integrate accounts of them into their belief systems. This study was the basis for my second book, Near-Death Experiences in Indigenous Religions (Oxford University Press, 2018).

As even the earliest NDE researchers discovered, no two NDEs are exactly alike. We know that the occurrence of NDEs is not due to expectation and prior religious beliefs, otherwise they would not happen to atheists and very young children. It's clear that we're not creating the experience, but our cultural backgrounds and our individuality act as filters for it. Even as we're experiencing it, our minds help to give it form and structure through the symbols and metaphors that help us to make sense of our reality. In other words, we're co-creating the experience, together with…whatever causes NDEs in the first place.

At this point, you may be wondering how my work fits in with the issue of NDEs as evidence for survival after death. Perhaps you may be wondering what conclusions

I've drawn from my research – if I believe that it supports the idea that NDEs are a genuine glimpse of the afterlife. And if so, what kind of afterlife could even be possible given all the diversity between accounts? I will return to these questions towards the end of the book, when I answer the question, "How has the near-death experience affected me?" For now, keep some of these issues tucked in the back of your mind as you embark on the journey that the following chapters will take you on.

SIX

Hard Statistics and Nuanced Observations

I regard consciousness as fundamental. I regard matter as derivative from consciousness. We cannot get behind consciousness. Everything that we talk about, everything that we regard as existing, postulates consciousness.

MAX PLANCK

While it might appear a bold statement, it is reasonable to conclude that all of the major components that occur during a near-death experience have already been revealed. From the early studies conducted by Raymond Moody, Peter Fenwick, and Pim van Lommel over 50 years ago to testimonials posted on YouTube yesterday, you will see a remarkable consistency of experience. And why wouldn't you? Heaven, or however you interpret this realm, is a destination that will not likely change. Whether advances in quantum mechanics give us more insights into this realm or not, the personal accounts that near-death experiencer's recount will not change.

This may sound disappointing as it relates to the possibility of new and more exciting revelations to come. However, if there were marked changes in experience, the mountain of data supporting the case for the existence of NDEs would actually weaken. It is precisely because the retelling of such experiences throughout human history have remained remarkably consistent that they carry such power and credibility.

And yet, if we shift our focus just slightly, we may open up different worlds of possibilities. The saying, "The devil is in the details" is an apt analogy. This saying was derived from an earlier phrase, more appropriate to our subject, "God is in the Details," which is an idiom that refers to a hidden element lurking in the fine elements. A deeper meaning that may not be evident at first glance.

Whether we interpret a near-death experience as literal or symbolic, it has an intensely deep meaning to all who visit this realm. It is, no doubt, a very different world. Is it literal? Is it symbolic? Is it both? This realm seems to communicate in the in between. In the language of metaphor. And this is not a language that lends itself easily to the scientific method.

It should be no surprise, therefore, that on our plain, we find extensive use of metaphor in the great religious and spiritual texts the world over. How else could we describe the ineffable, which a near-death experience embodies.

Metaphors are extremely powerful in that a well-placed object or expression will possess multiple shades of meaning. They manifest to speak to each person in a language they can relate to, and therefore more readily understand and assimilate. They navigate around our walls and penetrate our subconscious, imprinting a deeper meaning of something you may not normally have access to, in real-time.

Of course, a metaphor's meaning is subjective to the receiver, and its multi-layered symbolism will be seen and interpreted in the eye of the beholder. While there may be differences in interpretation, it is often in the struggle to understand and experience these metaphors that our own truths are revealed — where pieces of wisdom congeal — and where epiphanies are born.

Here is an example of a popular short tale, chock-full of metaphors which perfectly describes how those having experienced an NDE, in traveling the same path, may see, experience, and interpret them quite differently:

A group of blind men heard that a strange animal called an elephant had been brought to the town, but none of them were aware of its shape and form. Out of curiosity, they said, "We must inspect and know it by touch, of which we are capable." So, they sought it out, and when they found it, they groped about it. The first person, whose hand landed on the trunk, said, "This being is like a thick snake." For another one whose hand reached its ear, it seemed like a kind of fan. Another person, whose hand was upon its leg, said, "The elephant is a pillar like a tree-trunk." The blind man who placed his hand upon its side said the elephant "is a wall." Another, who felt its tail, described it as a rope. The last felt its tusk, stating the elephant is that which is hard, smooth, and like a spear.

While these blind men were all touching the same source, they each walked away with different perspectives of a shared truth, a similar concept to those who have encountered an NDE. When pulled together as one whole, we find the sum of their collective experience is worth more than the individual pieces. Where can we find the largest, most reliably measurable sampling of pieces to the NDE puzzle? In existing prospective and retrospective studies.

The focus and objective of a scientific study must be set well before its research begins. Once established, it must be strictly adhered to. New rules or standards cannot be applied along the way, lest the data be compromised. As it relates to near-death experience, the focus of the most cited studies has been more "big picture" in nature — the amount of people who have had an NDE, an out-of-body experience, or a life-review. How many have seen deceased loved ones, encountered a being of light, or visited a hellish realm? This makes sense. As recently as 50 years ago, the NDE was an almost unknown phenomenon. The more subtle nuances of a near-death experience have not been brought to the fore because they were not part of these studies' focus.

While we cannot return to past studies and pull out scientifically pure statistics, revisiting the data and drilling down in search of those nuances will likely yield new insights. And it is often the case that we learn as much about a subject by what we don't see. The near-death experience is no exception. In the chapters to follow, those qualities will be noted — a contrast that should provide greater context for that which we do know.

Just one example of this relates to who NDErs encounter in this realm. Thousands describe meeting loved ones and spiritual beings. However, there is one person in particular who is conspicuously missing in these encounters. It becomes glaringly clear when combing through the thousands of testimonials that are now documented. But for some reason this anomaly has not been discussed. Perhaps because it is something we are unsettled by.

The terms "prospective" and "retrospective" refer to the timing of data collection in a study. In prospective studies, individuals are followed over time, and data about them is collected as their characteristics or circumstances change. In retrospective studies, individuals are interviewed and information is collected about past events.

Each has their advantages and disadvantages. Prospective studies are generally considered " cleaner" and therefore more scientific. They are recorded soon after an event is identified, and as such, tend to have fewer potential sources of bias — including recall or misclassification bias that may leak into a retrospective study. Additionally, prospective studies generally gather larger amounts of data.

However, in the case of NDE research, it is in the retrospective studies that we find much more of the nuance that this book focuses on. And, to our good fortune, due to the unique qualities inherent in the near-death experience, the strength and validity of the data retrospective studies gather, and the conclusions that can be reasonably drawn in their analysis, puts them on firmer footing.

First and foremost, their sample size is now significantly

larger than those of prospective studies — the inverse of what is more common. And this advantage will only grow. An NDE is a rare outcome making a large prospective very difficult. And there is no assurance someone will be willing to freely disclose any or all aspects of their experience, or has had enough time to properly process it.

In a retrospective study, the subject is responding to or initiating contact with that study, which means they are more inclined to reveal greater detail. NDERF sets the standard in this regard. Their database contains over 5,000 testimonials, which were recorded utilizing a well-designed and thorough questionnaire that has remained virtually unchanged for the decades it has been in use.

Secondly, there are four inherent qualities, unique to a near-death experience, that "inoculates" the data, to a degree, from recall or misclassification bias:

1. NDE testimonials have remained remarkably consistent over decades — even millennia.

2. NDEs are universally described as "more real than real."

3. NDEs are so clear and powerful that they are remembered as if they had "just happened yesterday."

4. Those who have had an NDE state that the experience was the most significant event in their life. In short, the details of an NDE are not easily confused or forgotten — even over time.

———

From study to study, you will notice divergent results within certain categories in both the prospective and retrospective studies to follow. Why is this? There will always be a degree of variation in methodology utilized in the gathering of data from study to study. Questions posed about certain events experienced during an NDE, such as the out-of-body experience, will likely be worded differently, yielding different results. It is also possible that bias has some influence on outcomes. Even the most self-aware, responsible, and objective of researchers is not immune to this dynamic. However, with the tight focus of each of the prospective and retrospective studies, and the consistency in results within and against each other — even over a period of 27 years — it is reasonable to consolidate each of these types of studies into a more substantive and robust weighted average. Prospective to prospective. Retrospective to retrospective.

prospective study statistics

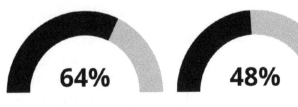

64%
an overwhelming
sense of peace

48%
heightened senses

45%
time - past / present
and future are one

39%
see deceased loved ones

38%
encounter spiritual beings

37%
have an
out-of-body experience

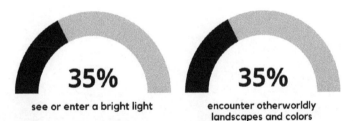

35%
see or enter a bright light

35%
encounter otherworldly
landscapes and colors

31%
enter a tunnel or path

25%
heightened understanding

20%
a border is reached

15%
experience a life-review

PROSPECTIVE

Year of Study	Pim van Lommel, et al. [1] 2001	Parnia, Fenwick, et al. [2] 2001	Schwaninger, et al. Schechtman, et al. [3] 2002	Greyson [4] 2003	
Number in study	344	63	30	105	542
Number having an NDE	62	4	7	11	84
Percent having an NDE	18%	6%	23%	10%	15.5%
					weighted average
an overwhelming sense of peace	56%	75%	100%	85%	64%
heightened senses		50%	54%	44%	48%
time - past/present/future are one		50%	9%	67%	45%
see deceased loved ones	32%	50%	72%	52%	39%
encounter spiritual beings		25%	63%	26%	38%
have and out-of-body experience	24%	50%	90%	70%	37%
see or enter a bright light	23%	75%	63%	70%	35%
otherworldly landscape and colors	29%	50%		63%	35%
enter a tunnel or path	31%				31%
heightened understanding		25%	18%	30%	25%
a border is reached	8%	100%	45%	41%	20%
experience a life-review	13%		9%	30%	15%

THE CIRCLE GRAPHS ARE DERIVED FROM A COMPILATION OF
1 2 3 4
THE FOUR MOST SITED PROSPECTIVE STUDIES ABOVE.

retrospective study frequency

77%

an overwhelming
sense of peace

65%

out-of-body experience

63%

time - past / present
and future are one

57%

heightened senses

56%

encounter otherworldly
landscapes and colors

51%

see or enter a bright light

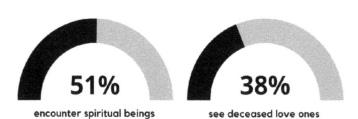

51%

encounter spiritual beings

38%

see deceased love ones

enter a tunnel or path

heightened understanding

a border is reached

experience a life-review

RETROSPECTIVE	Fenwick & Fenwick [5]	Long & Perry [6]	Greyson [7]	
Year of Study	**1997**	**2010**	**1983**	
Number of NDE cases in study	450	613	74	**1137**
				weighted average
an overwhelming sense of peace		76%	77%	**77%**
have and out-of-body experience	66%	75%	53%	**65%**
time - past/present/future are one		61%	64%	**63%**
heightened senses		74%	46%	**57%**
otherworldly landscape and colors		52%	58%	**56%**
see or enter a bright light		65%	43%	**51%**
encounter spiritual beings		57%	47%	**51%**
see deceased loved ones	38%	57%	26%	**38%**
enter a tunnel or path		34%	32%	**33%**
heightened understanding		31%	30%	**31%**
a border is reached	24%	31%	26%	**25%**
experience a life review	12%	22%	22%	**14%**

THE CIRCLE GRAPHS ARE DERIVED FROM A COMPILATION OF
5 6 7
THE THREE MOST SITED RETROSPECTIVE STUDIES ABOVE.

YOUR JOURNEY BEGINS

The otherworldly realm of the near-death experience is teeming with new and often strange sensations, from sights and sounds to core emotions. As you begin this journey, be on the lookout for the subtle details that are hiding just beneath the surface as well as the details you would expect to see that are not.

Before you read through the comments section at the end of each chapter, I would encourage you to put the book down, sit back, close your eyes, and absorb what you just read. Experience it. You may begin to see things in your mind's eye that are more revealing than what you may have noticed in the past. Remember, it is in the most minute details that we further our understanding of the greater whole.

The comments we present in Crossover are the nuances we have seen from our unique perspectives. You, no doubt, will see others that we do not, because your perspective is unique as well. Collectively, there will likely be many more gems to uncover, similar to a beachcomber sifting through a trillion grains of sand for that nugget of gold. Those nuances. The ones that exist below the obvious, or the common.

So let's begin our search for those nuances and see what we can sift out together.

SEVEN

The Out-of-Body Experience

Just as a little bird cracks open the shell and flies out, we fly out of this shell, the shell of the body. We call that death, but strictly speaking, death is nothing but a change in form.

SWAMI SATCHIDANANDA

At that precise moment, at an instant so brief it can't be measured, I disconnected from my body and was overflowed with a sense of fulfillment and weightlessness. I clearly understood that I had died and that I was free from all bother and heaviness, and I found myself alive and feeling wonderful with a sense of peace and incredible well-being. I was in a place of calm where I felt happy and euphoric to find that, yes, there is another life where death is no more.

When images of my wife and children came to me, I wasn't bothered by them, neither did I feel sorrow nor anything - because if what awaits them is this eternal wonder, of what importance is pain and suffering in this life if afterwards there is only peace and wellbeing? Such earthly problems and joys are seen as very insignificant from that realm. There is nothing to disturb the peace, and one feels love for all beings since there is no possibility of any rancor. It's a perfect state.

So there I was, happy and awaiting events knowing that someone would come to get me to enter into this eternal life, when I felt that I was returning to connect with my body and I began feeling the illness I had forgotten about.

The first thing I heard was a woman's voice with a Valencian accent saying, 'He's coming back, he's coming back!' Incredible peace and wellbeing, moved by immeasurable love for everything and everybody, bound by enormous joy and confirming the existence of another life. It is now knowledge where before it was only faith. It is by far the most powerful experience of my life. I now have no fear of death.[1]

At first, all I experienced was cold, and then my soul floated up out of my body. When I reached the level of the ceiling in my room, I turned around and saw my dead body on the bed. I felt a moment of regret, such as one might feel seeing a beautiful purebred dog dead on the side of the highway.

It was a good body, and it had served me well, but that

part of my existence was over with, and I was ready to move on. I did see the medical personnel who were scrambling to resuscitate me and I wished I could tell them not to bother. I turned around, looked up at the ceiling, and floated up into the plenum and through the roof of the building.[2]

Everything went black. I will never be able to remember how long it was that I could not see anything, but all of a sudden, I realized my eyes were open. There was one thing that didn't make sense; why was I floating? I was in the same spot that I had collapsed, but I was slightly higher up. Suddenly, I heard sirens and looked down.

I could see an ambulance with people coming out. They were putting me on a stretcher. I heard one man say, 'This man has no chance of survival. He has been here without any help for nearly an hour!' The other man said, 'I'm sure he is already dead. I didn't realize it was this bad.' I could see everything so clearly.I wasn't feeling any pain and actually felt very comfortable..... I became curious. What would happen if I continued to float up? I began to go up, up, and up.[3]

The next thing I remember is coming out of my body. I was floating up towards the ceiling of the operating room and toward the light. At that point, it was just the bright lights in the operating room. I looked down and saw my body with many people around it. I did not feel any attachment to my body or regret upon leaving it. I felt mildly curious as to what they were all doing. I decided it was really none of my concern.

I felt so light and free: free of the pain of the past several weeks and free of the pain of my life up to that point. I felt like I had nothing too important to keep me from leaving, especially since my body had been nothing but a source of pain. I felt more than ready to go. I continued floating up and out of the hospital. I saw the city and all the people going about their business.

The higher I floated, the people and places growing smaller and smaller until I could see the earth itself growing smaller and smaller. I began to feel and see a complete connection to everyone, every creature, every plant, every rock - everything. I could see how we are all connected, part of each other, and part of God.

I felt so much love. I felt a joy that is indescribable. I really don't have the words to describe how completely joyful, perfect, whole, and part of everything I felt and knew. Before I died, I questioned everything. Here, I knew everything and there were no more questions.[4]

All at once, I heard one of the nurses yell out, 'Straight line, straight line, my God! We've got a straight line!' At that exact moment, it was as if my consciousness was sucked into a vacuum. And everything became crystal clear. My knowledge of 'someone' being operated on became a knowledge of knowing it was me that was being operated on - that it was my heart that had just stopped beating. And the thing of it was - I was aware of it all.

I had full knowledge of the fact that my body had just stopped living. I could hear lots of commotion in the operating room (even though I was completely sedated and with no heartbeat). The nurses that were assisting were quite frantic.[5]

One of the guys doing CPR kept looking up, and I thought he was looking right at me. He kept calling me to take a breath. Eventually I'd be overcome with compassion and go back and take a breath, and then I would leave again. It was very interesting to talk to him later, because we were both equally irritated with each other. I wanted to strangle him because he was interfering with my progress, and he wanted to strangle me because I would take a breath, and then I'd stop breathing again! And the cycle would keep going.

So it was interesting to corroborate that sequence of events later. I was also absolutely overcome by the sense of being home, of being where I truly belonged. And I was surprised by the fact that I was not coming back. I love my husband dearly. I love my children more than I could ever imagine loving something on earth. But in comparison to God's love, the love I feel here is pale. I mean, I was home. I knew I'd had a great life to that point, and I was surprised that I had absolutely no desire to return.

I still feel a little guilty saying that. I didn't talk about this for many years partly because until my kids were old enough, I would not have wanted them to hear me say that. Out of context and before you have understanding — for a kid to think that they're not enough of a reason to come back is terrible. But at that point, I could hardly wait to get to the threshold of God's kingdom of heaven.[6]

I started humming and as I heard myself humming I also heard a nurse say 'We're losing her; her blood pressure is down to... she's dying.' I remember thinking 'Someone's dying in this room - I wonder who it is?' I wanted to lift my head to see, but couldn't. Then suddenly the pain stopped and I remember thinking 'Thank God, they gave me something.'

Slowly I started floating backwards off the table. I could see the big clock on the wall and all the doctors and nurses around me. There was frantic activity. Every detail of the emergency room was crystal clear.[7]

Very quickly, I started losing touch with this world. I knew without a doubt that I was in the process of dying. I was examining the feeling in a non-emotional, interested way. I was surprised to find that the closer I got to death the less I hurt and found that death was a relief and not the painful experience I always thought it would be. I then felt that I left this world and my body and was in the presence of God/ Jesus.[8]

Soon, all feeling ceased, but I realized I was floating around the room looking down at my body. I had an opportunity to look closely into the face of each person working on me. By this time, there was intense panic in the operating room, but yet, I felt peaceful.

I seemed to have a heart connection to each person there, especially with the anesthesiologist. She was terrified and working hard to bring me back into my body. I didn't want to get back into my body. ... Now I was inside another awareness. My memories are as vivid today as they were at the time. I knew I was dead to the earth, but I was just fine with that possibility. I actually felt very comfortable, with no longing or panic to return. I had no questions, only complete acceptance. It was peaceful, comfortable, and I felt very safe.

The facts have been checked out. I saw and heard all the medical staff in the operating room talking and working on my body. I heard my surgeon directing all the life-saving practices. I watched nurses put some kind of elastic leggings on my legs and hook me up to monitors. I saw and felt all the emotions in the room. I flew around and looked directly at each person and learned what they were thinking while they worked on me.

I still remember all of that vividly. I have verified with the help of the surgeon, who later became a friend, that my knowledge of each person was accurate, and he confirmed that I was correct about what he was doing and thinking and saying. I clearly left my body and existed outside it.[9]

The doctor stopped in the big hospital hall and asked himself if they should immediately go to the operating room. High in the hall shone a warm golden, yellow light. Slowly but surely, I was being sucked toward the light. The doctor gently struck my face and called my name. Then I realized then that the girl on the stretcher was me. I got super-excited saying to myself, 'I'm in death, this is death!'

I couldn't bear the thought that people on Earth don't understand death and that we go on living but without a body. I wanted to tell all the people on Earth that death isn't death and that there is more. But I kept moving further from the Earth and toward the light. I looked towards the Earth and had compassion for all people. I felt sorrow for them, that they didn't know. That they were ignorant as they suffered and argued on earth.[10]

And all the while, during this commotion, it was as if I had been immersed into some kind of essence or form of energy that I can only describe as the purest form of 'love' that there is. It was an incredibly wonderful feeling. It was as if my soul had been blended with the soul of what we perceive to be God. There was no distinguishing where I began or where I ended. In other words, I wasn't in a body.

I was in, around and part of an immense and wondrously overwhelming sensation of love and under-standing. And I was completely at ease. Even though I realized what had taken place from a physical standpoint, I had absolutely no worries about ANY of the consequences to the end of the physical living. I was in a completely different place. And it was just SO much more wonderful a place to be. I wanted to remain there. The feeling was utter peace, tranquility, bliss, love. All at the same time!

The words simply pale in comparison to the feeling, and are incapable of describing how wonderful it felt being 'where' I was. Why would ANYONE not want to stay there? (I get goose bumps talking about this.)[11]

After suffering a gunshot wound to the chest, I was unconscious when I arrived at the emergency room. Within minutes, I was in shock and dying. Suddenly I was looking down on my body and the crowd of doctors and nurses working to revive me.

I looked around and found that I was up above the room and in the very left-hand corner of the 'picture'. Looking to my right, I could see a brilliant light as if it were coming from behind a door an indefinite distance away. I wanted to go through the door but could not because of what the doctors were doing. Now they were putting tubes into my chest and I yelled at them to 'Leave her alone, let her go, stop hurting her!' repeatedly.

I no longer saw that person, that body as being me, but as a separate entity. Yet, unless they let that entity die, I could not live to go through the door to the light. I felt no pain, no fear and my emotions were calm but I felt an urgency to get to the light because the door was slowing closing.Suddenly a shock opened my eyes and I was back inside that wounded body again in the intensive care unit. I felt a terrible loss inside.

While I considered myself looking into the room, I was also looking across a universe of space to the light behind the open door I needed to reach before it closed. I was seeing the people from above and at eye level at the same time; I could read their name tags, even smell their breath. I moved among them and through them without touching them. It was like watching the same show from ten different camera angles.[12]

This time I opened my eyes, I was not in a hospital, but somewhere else. It's hard to explain, but it felt like a room where there were no colors, no walls, and no darkness. But the room did have a color. It was the color of light.

I had no thoughts of my children, my family, and there were no cars, birds, trees, nothing. I knew something was wrong. I felt that I was dead, but it was, like, not even a worry, like I didn't even care. Then I noticed the light was coming only from one direction - the direction I was looking. There was no side view, only straight-ahead tunnel vision. I had to turn my head to see what I wanted to see. Whatever direction I looked in, that's the direction I went in. If I wanted to get from where I was to somewhere else, all I had to do was look, and I was there.

I remember after learning that, looking down to see how fast my legs were moving. But there were no legs, no arms, no body, no nothing! I felt as though I was just vision, a set of eyes. But there were no eyes, either. No words were spoken that I heard. It was as if I was so amazed at moving so fast and turning my head to see, and finding myself float-ing. Whenever I wasn't moving, I felt as if I was floating.

I noticed that the things I was learning about the place I was in just popped into my mind. I don't know where my body was or how I was able to see or feel. I felt as if I could have spoken, but I don't even know how I was able to think. But I WAS thinking things like this, 'I don't know about her [that nurse.] Here's this guy is dying, and you're worried about a little throw-up on you. Get out of here!"[13]

I left my body as my husband pulled under the awning of the emergency room. I saw them take me out of the vehicle and put me into a wheelbarrow chair looking thing. I saw the way each of the workers looked and what they were wearing. I saw my husband off to the side as I began to float farther and farther up. Then, I just saw their legs under the awning, the top of the hospital, and the mall to the side.

It looked like I was floating into a huge light that looked like the full moon. It was cold outside but I was perfectly warm. I was still wearing my clothes as I floated out because as I looked down and saw my legs, they were clad with the same clothes I had been wearing. Then all of a sudden, I was rapidly sucked into what I thought was this full moon. That night the moon was a sliver, so this was 'the light' that NDErs talk about.[14]

I stopped breathing and almost immediately my heart stopped. Then, I left. Suddenly, I opened my eyes and I felt totally liberated, I saw myself in a hospital gown, with the doctors around my body trying to resuscitate me. I saw how they were busily moving from one place to another, each time smaller and more distant.

The sensation was strange because I felt myself complete integral and without doubt, I saw my inert body in front of me. I floated alone. No one tried to hold down my painful legs and arms. The relief was enormous. I couldn't control that which had happened, I let go. Then, there began the most wonderful journey.[15]

I felt completely well and comfortable floating up above. I didn't have any wounds or feel any pain. All that I felt was joy and peacefulness. In that split second, my soul had come out from my body, floating up on top of the glider in the air, watching myself dying. That was an incredible feeling!

At the point of death, my body and soul separated. 'I' was in dual existence. When my soul came out of my body, I felt like a new being, leaving behind all my old senses, thoughts, and emotions. I could still see, hear, and feel the surrounding world, and was self-aware of my inner mind. However, the cognitive processes were remarkably different. While body exists in a physical form, in that capacity I no longer had any bodily boundaries or physical limitations.[16]

Coworkers found me not breathing and in cardiac arrest. I am white, but my skin color was purple and black from lack of oxygen. They gave me chest compressions while an ICU doctor intubated me by having to lie down on his stomach on the floor. Apparently, they placed me on a backboard and ran with me to an ICU room. That's when I popped out of my body and watched EVERY single CPR and medical procedure done to me.

I heard and saw it ALL. It was a distinctive 'pop' that I felt when I left my body. I was on the ceiling watching it all. I didn't really feel disturbed to see my body on the bed. I just thought that I looked terrible and 'no way am I going back into that!'

I watched coworkers do chest compressions and cut off my clothes and thought, 'Dammit, that was my best Victoria's Secret bra.' I heard staff members calling out my labs, and thinking, 'Hmmm, that's not good, she's not gonna make it.' I watched blood being drawn and a central line being inserted into my groin. I saw my blood splash all over the doctor, which I did feel badly about.

I saw coworkers checking my pupils, saying they were fixed and dilated. I could see from the ceiling that they were correct. I watched the whole CPR medication protocol followed, and so much more. I have a VERY expensive 5-carat diamond ring from my husband, which a nurse removed for safekeeping. I remember thinking, 'The only way that's coming off is off of my cold dead hand.'

Then realizing, 'Oh yeah, I am dead, so...' I had two emergency beepers in my nursing scrub pocket. One was the CPR beeper. I remember hearing it going off as my CPR was being called overhead. As they were cutting off my scrub top, I remember thinking, 'Well I'm not responding to this one.[17]

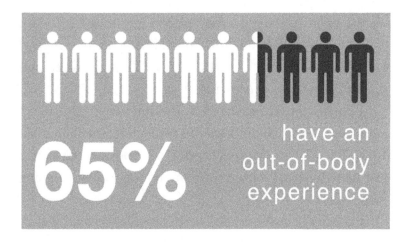

Crossover Retrospective Compilation[18]

OBSERVATIONS

DJ Kadagian

• Those having an out-of-body experience (OBE) most often find themselves floating directly above the operating table looking down on their bodies — not standing or floating to the side. In transitioning to this state, they often express pain at being pulled or "wrenched" out of their bodies while experiencing an intense compression. This feeling is generally short-lived and there is relief from any pain they were suffering just prior to their NDE.

• There is a very clear realization that they have died, along with a loss of physical and emotional connection with their body. They begin to understand it as separate from who they are in their new manifestation. Some express appreciation for how their body served them during their earthly incarnation, while others are happy to shed a form they feel is constricting, dense, or a source of chronic pain.

• There is rarely a "fight" to survive or to hang on to this life. On the contrary, more often they attempt to communicate to the medical staff to stop trying to resuscitate them — oftentimes shouting, but to no avail as they cannot be heard. This contrasts with their ability to hear what is being said and even thought by the medical team.

• A high percentage of those who have an OBE speak in great detail about what is happening around their body during attempts to resuscitate them — from the procedures and dialogue of the medical staff to the sounds and visual signals produced by the medical equipment. Surprisingly, they appear to focus as much attention on the staff as their own bodies.

• NDErs reactions range from concern for the staff's emotional state to amusement at the whole situation and how frantic they are in their efforts to bring them back from a place they would much rather be. Many doctors and nurses later confirm the events described by NDErs during the OBE.

• It is common for someone knowingly approaching death over a more extended period of time, whether in a hospital, hospice or at home, to experience a bedside apparition or visitation from deceased loved ones or spiritual beings. They appear to be entering a stage of preparation where they are drifting between our physical world and the next. The beings they often encounter are comforting and appear to be helping them prepare for the transition. In contrast, those experiencing an OBE during an NDE do not see deceased loved ones or spiritual beings in the hospital room.

• It is common to hear NDErs express that they are not concerned with leaving their families. They now know their loved ones have so much to look forward to when they pass, while also understanding that, in the grand scheme of things, their time on earth is very brief. After their NDE, they often express surprise, and in some cases guilt, at having had this feeling. Some will not divulge this to a loved one as it might be misinterpreted or misunderstood.

Gregory Shushan, PhD.

• The concern for the experience to be externally validated seems to recur quite often. Many accounts stress that some aspect of their experience is proven by some sort of corroboration — either from a doctor, or something they observed that was later confirmed. A good example is a Huguenot minister named L.J. Bertrand, who had an NDE after nearly freezing to death while climbing in the Swiss Alps in 1861. When he recounted his NDE, he was very careful to stress the elements that proved to him that it was real, such as seeing his wife board a different train than the one she'd planned on taking in a city miles away, and one of the guides sneaking off with Bertrand's lunch.

• There are often feelings of disgust at the corpse they are now viewing from above. In a quote from Bertrand's account: "There is the corpse in which I lived and which I called me, as if the coat were the body, as if the body were the soul! What a horrid thing is that body! — deadly pale, with a yellowish blue color, holding a cigar in its mouth and a match in its two burned fingers! Well, I hope that you shall never smoke again, dirty rag!"

Dr. Pim van Lommel

• This out-of-body experience is scientifically important because doctors, nurses, and relatives can verify the reported perceptions, and they can also corroborate the precise moment the NDE with OBE occurred during the period of CPR. In two reviews with a total of more than 200 corroborated reports of potentially verifiable out-of-body perceptions, it was found that about 98 percent of the reported OBEs were completely accurate. Through verification, it was proven that all reported perceptions during coma, cardiac arrest, or general anesthesia were about details that actually happened. Based on these veridical aspects, an OBE can, by definition, not be a hallucination, because this means experiencing a perception that has no basis in "reality" like in psychosis, neither it can be a delusion, which is an incorrect assessment of a correct perception, nor an illusion, which means a misleading image.[19]

• For many people, the overwhelming feelings of peace, joy, and bliss constitute the first and best-remembered element of their experience. The intense pain that usually follows a traffic accident or heart attack is suddenly completely gone.[20]

• It is often confusing to hear bystanders or doctors declare them dead at a moment when they feel extremely alive and whole. [21]

• If a sound is heard at this point, it is usually a buzzing or whistling sound. Sometimes, a loud click or a soft murmur is noticed instead.

• Patients feel as if they have taken off their body like an old coat and they are astounded that despite discarding it, they have retained their identity with the faculty of sight, with emotions, and with an extremely lucid consciousness

• The most common vantage point is from the ceiling, and because of this unusual position, some people initially fail to recognize their bodies. To their utter amazement, they go unnoticed even though they can hear and see everything themselves.

• The range of their vision can extend to 360 degrees with simultaneous detailed and bird's eye views. Blind people have the faculty of sight while deaf people know exactly what is being said.

• This out-of-body experience is of scientific importance because doctors, nursing staff, and relatives can check and corroborate the reported perceptions and the moment when they were supposed to have taken place.

• Regarding an apparition at the bedside, this occurs from your physical body while you are still conscious. In an end-of-life experience, you can see your deceased mother, father, or partner coming to comfort or take you with them. So, you are still seeing them out of the position of your own body. When you are out of your body during a near-death experience, you are no longer conscious. Brain functioning has ceased. As such, you are in another, higher dimension — another local realm, where you can meet deceased relatives.

EIGHT

The Tunnel Experience

The grave is but a covered bridge leading from light to light, through a brief darkness!

HENRY WADSWORTH LONGFELLOW

I hovered over the left shoulder of my surgeon and remained there until something pulled me completely away from the operating room. I felt an intense squeezing sensation in my head and felt a huge pain as I heard a shrill loud sound. It lasted a few seconds, and then I felt complete peace.

What I experienced was like being sucked out of the operating room through a tiny pin-dot of light. As my 'eyes' adjusted to the space, I seemed to see tiny pin-dots of light everywhere in front of me. I realized I was sitting in a comfortable chair moving toward those pin dots, and they were getting larger. Eventually, one of them grew into a huge beacon of brilliant white light, glowing at me as I moved closer and closer.

I felt myself watching with amusement as I was pulled inside the light in an easy chair. I realized someone was with me. It seemed like it was a man, but I never really knew. The Being was communicating with me through thoughts; no talking and no need to use words. It happened so fast! Now I was inside another awareness. My memories are as vivid today as they were at the time.[1]

I estimate the size of this tunnel to be a diameter of six to seven feet. I could stand without touching the top. My height was five foot ten inches...... Finally, I stopped moving through the tunnel and had a good chance to look at it. The tunnel looked like a large vent pipe used on clothes dryers. The light was not primarily inside the tunnel but from the outside shining in. During the trip inside the tunnel, I heard a loud buzzing sound, which hurt my ears. I wondered what supported the tunnel. Now I began walking looking for the ending of this tunnel.[2]

...there were little doorways all along this tunnel and I felt that I could, if I wanted to, go into any of those doorways. I felt at the time that if I did I would not come back....[3]

I left my body and floated above it while observing the fruitless efforts of the many people below who were trying to revive me. As my earthly senses disappeared, I began seeing images of others and people who had passed away. I seemed to float upwards or outwards and experienced a parabolic worm hole in space. As I passed through the wormhole, I emerged into a vast darkness with many small points of light.

There came an understanding that each point of light was an individual entity like myself. All were exactly similar and had no connection to their life as a human being. A brighter light appeared some distance in space or time. When drawn to this greater light, images of my family appeared.[4]

The tunnel was made of brown bricks, about the size of regular house bricks. I got the impression of wetness or shininess on the bricks in the tunnel. But when I touched the bricks, which I did as I was advancing upwards in the tunnel, they were not wet.[5]

I'm in a 'tunnel' that's ox-blood red, it's narrow or sort of 'close'. I kind of float ahead through windings and curves, but I never hit anything. It feels warm, peaceful and pleasant and it's just like 'everything runs smoothly'.[6]

As I headed to the light, I could sense there was something on my right. I don't know what it was, but I could sense it in some way. I never looked away from the light. I knew if I could get past the doorway, that I could stay forever. As I approached the light, I could feel that emotional blend getting stronger and stronger. Before I could cross the threshold, everything went black again.[7]

The visual area was a combination of massive space and definitive location. To explain: I saw a tunnel from the outside as I was floating in space from several thousand feet above it. The space all around me was the color of a warm soft sky blue. There were wisps of soft white light moving within my visual range, and far off in the distance.

The tunnel appeared as translucent blue and white and it seemed as though I could look through it. The tunnel opening was below me yet the tunnel itself flowed up and way above my visual plane and merged into a beautiful blue and white light where everything came together. It was the most incredible view I have ever seen in my life. I could feel this area around me and it seemed comforting and safe.

The tunnel was large with soft rounded edges flowing into it. It was soft blue in color, not claustrophobic but warm and comforting, inviting. As I entered the space around the entrance, I floated in and started to move forward.[8]

The tunnel/path had silhouettes of beings on the other side of some undefined boundary. I could hear sounds but not intelligible. This place was free of pain and I felt I was one with all. I had arrived to a place without pain. My vision was 360 degrees it was profoundly beautiful.[9]

It suddenly became easier to breathe. I knew everything the doctor was about to do, before he did things. I began to ascend, face first, through a tunnel that was a warm, reddish color, like the color of tomato soup, but soft and similar to clouds. There was an unearthly golden white light at the end, but not very near. I was concerned about my son at home and the son I was having. I knew I was dead but wasn't concerned about that so much. Instantly it was made known to me that they would be all right. It was very reassuring.[10]

I found myself traveling through a tunnel of sorts at lightning speed, sort of like the 'Star Wars' movie 'time warp.' It was as though all energy of the universe was passing by me, and soon there were specks of bright white light converging into a glaring white light. It felt like a rocket-propelled orgasm. This feeling was like no other I had experienced and like no other I have experienced since then - it was as if providence was holding me.[11]

Immediately I was hurling along the tunnel much faster than I wished. The speed was tremendous. I was scared. Somewhere along my journey in this tunnel, I slowed to a stop and a man calmed me and told me the trip was nearing an end. Away I went again at the same speed as before. I do not know how I survived the trip. The speed had to be at the speed of light or even faster. I felt no g-forces, only fear and the exhilaration of a terrible speed.[12]

As I looked at the tunnel entrance, I moved at the speed of thought immediately to the opening of this tunnel. I think more, I was drawn to it by nature or fate as if I knew what to do.[13]

I was walking on a pathway with flowing water on either side of me. There was a tunnel, the entrance of which was somewhat dark, but as I began to walk through it, it became brighter. And at the end of the tunnel, there was this over-whelmingly bright light...

I entered the tunnel, and as I walked further into it, I could see some cloudy figures, like indistinct shadows of people. But then there was one that I just knew was my mother, who had passed. I'm not sure how I knew it was her. It reminds me of when you suddenly smell something, which vividly brings back a memory of the past. I was an adult, but I could hear myself call her 'Mommy.'

She took my hand and led me to the edge of the tunnel

and into the light; and I could see green rolling fields that seemed to go on forever, and a sky so blue. The colors were like nothing that I had ever seen before. There was this wonderful, overwhelming sense of peace. We talked, but without moving our mouths i.e. without words. How to say this? We communicated through our thoughts.

The colors and sounds were so vivid! There were variously colored, transparent orbs that seemed to pulsate. There were many that I could describe as 'mystical beings' there. The whole experience was mystical to me.[14]

I was moving head first through a dark m'lstrom of what looked like black boiling clouds, feeling that I was being beckoned to the sides, which frightened me.[15]

I felt like I was walking through the tunnel without feeling my feet on the ground, walking quickly, and there were others walking with me. They mostly walked single file, but at least two other people walked together side by side.[16]

I was in a completely dark tunnel. There was no floor. I was floating. At the end, I saw a very small light. I heard voices in the distance but couldn't understand what they said. It was like being in a library where you hear people speaking softly. There was an incredible scent of red roses. I began to walk and walk and walk. I wanted to get to the light because it would take me to a special place.

I noticed I wasn't getting any closer to the light and I began to raise my hands. I began praying and said, 'Lord, my soul praises and glorifies you. Help me God. I want to get to the light and I can't.' Suddenly I did.[17]

I did not see myself getting out of my body nor floating above it, I just remember going into a wide and long tunnel, like entering a train tunnel. At the beginning, there was still earthly light. Then I entered darkness, which was not a complete event, as if it was getting denser and denser, and it filled the whole arch. The darkness was indeed not black but rather dark grey and thick in its outlines, dense; in the center, the void was clear. ..At the end of this tunnel, I saw this beautiful, extremely attractive light, and to which I came closer very fast.[18]

After 'blacking out,' I suddenly awoke in a tunnel. The tunnel was rotating and was giving off a metallic clanking sound for each rotation. The walls of the tunnel were light gray, probably even a pearl color. It was divided into sections by round 'ribs' of a darker color. In the tunnel it was not dark, but at the end of the tunnel there was a round exit, beyond which a brighter white light could be seen.

I didn't float anywhere but stayed in place. There were

geometrical figures, mostly spheres, passing around me and going off into the distance. I thought, 'Where am I?' and 'Who am I?' I could not at all remember who I was; I didn't even remember that I was a person! The next question was 'What am I?' But I didn't see that I had a body because there wasn't any body! But I was thinking, which meant that I was alive.

I started to slowly move deeper into the tunnel to where the spheres were going.How interestingly everything was arranged here. I understood that life is arranged in the same way. My thoughts were very rapid and 'crystal-clear.' I felt as if I knew everything. I was able to receive an answer to any question that I had. Then I heard a voice that said, 'Well, is that enough?' 'But she's thrashing about,' another voice objected. And with tremendous speed I was pulled back into my body and I woke up.[19]

The doctor returned, induced labor, and the birth pains became so excruciating that there were loud crashing noises and cymbals inside my body and head. Then there was a loud scraping noise similar to a pipe being pulled from another tighter pipe.

As unusual as it is, my soul left my body and I flew through space in a tunnel with lights streaking on each side (my soul left my feet and proceeded upward through my head and out). I flew thousands of miles per second and felt protected from evil and harm by the colorful lights. At the end of the tunnel was a light, which was Jesus' robe.[20]

Suddenly, I saw total black. I couldn't see anything. I started to panic, and yelled, "Hello!" I didn't get a response. Then, I called out to a higher power, and suddenly, I saw immense light. I was able to float towards that light. As I entered, I realized that I was getting sucked into some vortex. Then, I was in a cave or a tunnel. I could see the same light, but it was at the end of this tunnel. I started to float towards that light, and I came closer, and closer. As I got to the end, with a door. This door had typical Islamic ornamentation on it. The door opened, and it looked absolutely dark. However, this was only for a few seconds.[21]

Yes a tunnel with wandering souls in the form of shades at the entry, and at the end a light. From the moment I entered the tunnel, I changed dimension and my vibratory rate was changing. People that don't enter the tunnel, are persons staying with the physical energy of earth. They cannot change their vibratory rate because of their physical past they are unable to let go.[22]

Suddenly, with a physical shock, I was out of my body, standing, alone, in a gray darkness. I stood there for a bit and looked around, but while I could see my naked body and feet, I couldn't make out anything else. I remember saying, 'God, is this where I am going to spend eternity?'

Suddenly, to my left, I could make out a 'cave?' (Best way I can put it) entrance which was as dark as anything I had ever seen. I really had a feeling of fear and apprehension and knew I didn't want to go there. At about the same time I had a sense of absolute peace and also saw a 'path' leading off and up to the right which had begun to get lighter.

I began 'moving', not walking, just moving, like on the moving walkways in some airports towards that path. The 'grayness' I was in was absolutely, totally, 'gray' but had depth and seemed to go on forever. Not like being in a dense fog where you have some sense of 'closeness' to the fog. More like looking out into space and seeing nothing. I can't even verbalize it. Although I knew I was standing upright, I didn't have a sense of being supported by anything; I guess I was floating but it didn't seem like that, either. I was just 'there'. I also remember vaguely wondering if this was Limbo. I knew Catholics had the theory of Limbo, but I never knew exactly what it was or thought too much about it. In looking at the 'cave', I was also aware that it was totally and absolutely black. I can still vividly picture it in my mind and the sight of it comes to mind often.

It was really a bad place and I thank God I did not make a trip there, even for a visit... I saw the black hole and the light coming down the tunnel. I related that to a friend, and she said, 'I didn't think you could choose where you wanted to go.' My reply was, 'My sense is, we chose where we go by the life we live while on the earth.' I absolutely believe that was what I was shown.[23]

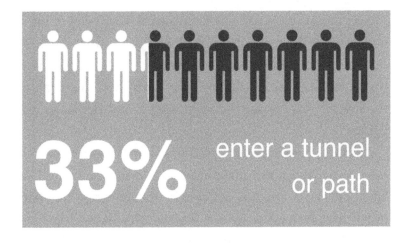

OBSERVATIONS

DJK

• The tunnel experience presents the widest range of emotion during a near-death experience, perhaps because it is often the first experience in this otherworldly realm they encounter — and it is a place where they begin to orient themselves.

• Whether transitioning into the tunnel from an out-of-body experience or finding themselves in the tunnel directly after clinical death, their feelings range from the positive — an overwhelming sense of peace, unconditional love, or feeling as if they are "finally home" — to the negative:

confusion, disorientation, and fear, which is much less common.

• The physical characteristics of the tunnel NDErs describe vary widely. The most common colors are pitch black, a deep red, gray, or a bluish hue. The tunnel may be solid and opaque, amorphous, and translucent, rough or smooth, shiny and wet or dry to the touch. Of note, very few who experience an NDE attempt feeling the interior surface of the tunnel. In such an otherworldly and novel space, one would expect this to happen more often than described.

• It is difficult to gauge the tunnel's overall size as descriptions vary widely. On balance, we are left with the impression that it is roundish in shape, not too wide, and with a flat, uncluttered path. While it is rarely reported as large or cavernous, its length is too broadly described to estimate. It is not generally described as winding from left to right or up and down. It appears to be stable, although some have described it as vibrating or undulating. While it does not seem to create noise itself, those who have reported sounds tend to describe them in more unpleasant terms — buzzing, clanking, or shrill.

• NDErs most often describe experiencing the tunnel from within, although some have reported viewing the tunnel from the outside. Movement towards the end of the tunnel may be slow or at lightning speed, by foot or floating, but in most cases, there is a sense they are being pulled or drawn towards the light that is most often reported at its end, as opposed to the NDEr being in control and actively engaged in moving towards that destination.

• While we most often associate the tunnel with a bright

light at its endpoint, very often the NDEr will describe brilliant white "pin-dots" all around them within, or at the end
of the tunnel.

• The tunnel has been described by some as looking and
feeling as if they are in a wormhole. Interestingly, for those
intrigued by the science of the NDE, this wormhole
description might hint at quantum mechanics's interpretation of movement between space, time, and even dimension. Is the tunnel NDErs encounter much more than their
description reveals? Does this tunnel transport NDErs to a
far-off part of the universe, or even a different dimension?
While NDErs know they are moving away from earth, we
rarely hear where they think they are going, or where they
believe they are located when they arrive.

• Beings encountered in the tunnel, which is not uncommon, are never people they knew on this plain, who are still
alive. They are deceased loved ones, people they don't
recognize, or spiritual beings. In many cases, they have
encountered people they thought to still be alive who had
already crossed over. In most cases, there is the sense these
beings are there to greet and guide them on the first leg of
their journey.

GS

• The tunnel is one of the main examples of an NDE
feature that is *not* commonly found across cultures. There
was a debate about this between arch-skeptic Susan Blackmore and Allan Kellehear. Blackmore wanted to see NDE

content as purely universal because it aligned with her theory that NDEs are just the result of a dying brain. Because if it's a dying brain, culture should not be a factor — the human brain should function the same way in any culture.

• Kellehear convincingly argued that the tunnel is merely symbolic of entering darkness and emerging into light — descriptions of which are numerous in indigenous societies. Indeed, many narratives described traveling through dark or narrow passageways leading to brightly-lit realms, including chasms, canyons, trees, caves, houses, forests, or some unspecified "darkness" or "gloom" as well as actual tunnels. In other words, NDErs in the west commonly experience/interpret/describe the experience of transitioning through a place of darkness and into light as a "tunnel." This helps account for the differences in descriptions of the tunnel. It's as if a person's memories and mental databanks are overlaying the objective NDE elements with understandable, relatable imagery.

• Some ancient people believed that the stars or pin lights often described were souls of the dead. The belief that stars are souls of the dead is fairly common. In ancient Egypt and Greece, souls could become "Imperishable Stars" — they had become divinized. They were specifically the circumpolar stars, meaning they were given a physical location. In the ancient Vedic Indian text, Shatapatha Brahmana, the souls of the righteous became stars in the heavenly realm. Likewise, in the ancient Chinese text Zhuangzi, some advanced spirits became stars. In the Maya myth, Popol Vuh, the hero twins become stars in the sky after their underworld adventures. Nahua people believed that the souls of warriors became stars. In ancient Greek mythology, the souls of heroes became gods. Similar beliefs are found among the Gilgulim Inuit and the Mbuti of the Congo Ituri rainforest. The Bakongo of the Lower Congo believed that shooting stars were souls of the dead. The Maori similarly believed that souls of the dead descended to the underworld as shooting stars.

PvL

• The tunnel experience is the crossing from the physical realm to the nonlocal realm where everything and everybody is connected, all is ONE, past and future are available, it is beyond time and space, and there is unconditional love. People feel HOME. This sensation of moving through a tunnel toward the light has become almost synonymous with near-death experiencers.

   • People move through this dark, occasionally multi-colored or spiral-shaped narrow space, sometimes accompanied by visible or invisible beings or by music.[25]

   • Usually, deceased relatives are met in the other, higher dimension, and not in the tunnel which is extremely rare.

NINE

Into the Light(s)

I believe that when death closes our eyes we shall awaken to a light, of which our sunlight is but the shadow.

ARTHUR SCHOPENHAUER

It suddenly, it seemed like the light surrounding everything got even brighter, if that's possible, until I could no longer see the hospital equipment, nor the intensive care unit, nor the partition, nor my body or hear anything any human being said. Only light existed, without limits or dullness or anything to contain it, without point of emission, light upon light that didn't come from any source nor go to any place. Light filled everything and everything was light, including me.

I then felt accompanied by others, as if I were the protagonist of the universe, as if every living being had all at once decided I was their focus of love. I thought, 'I have asked myself my whole life what pure love is, and it turns out that love is light.' I wanted it never to end, and it occurred to me that something so great couldn't have an end.[1]

What happened next was the slowly spinning white light that came towards me a very clear and pure light that had fine white and gold tendrils off of it and this white light came towards me and the best part about it is it came packaged with a perfect musical melody ...

As this pure white light came towards me it was coming with this perfect musical melody absolutely beautiful and as you will hear sound music vibration frequency is the way that our souls transcended in these levels it's one of the reasons why sound hymns chants had been used for thousands of years to help engender deep transcendental conscious states in any kind of spiritual broadening of consciousness religious.[2]

I could see a pinpoint of white light in front of me in the distance the size of a pencil eraser head, that size. So, I sensed that I start moving in that direction; but it felt like something was pulling me there, I don't feel as if I was doing it. At this point, I was like floating to and upright position. Then going slowly towards that pinpoint of light.[3]

I looked up at what I thought was the sky. I could see all these stars and they were so beautiful. I continued looking at them and reaching out towards them and saying how beautiful they were. The stars were so bright, but I could look at them without being blinded. Then some of the stars started coming towards me.

I turned to the presence on the side of me and said how beautiful they were and that I wished they would hurry up and get closer. When I turned back to look at the stars, they were in the forms of crosses. I thought they were the most beautiful things I had ever seen and I was so happy. I really felt as though they were angels coming for me.[4]

I started to float but could not tell in which direction. I was gradually able to make out a small light and noticed that I was quickly traveling toward it through what seemed like a big tunnel. My arrival there is a little confusing. I was welcomed by beings who I remember as very tall and made of an incredible light. They loved me like no one had ever loved me.

I felt what can only be described as the love of God surrounding me, welcoming me, filling me with warmth and happiness. To this day, when the suffering of this world makes me despair, I close my eyes and travel there. The fact that all of this will pass and I will return with them is a consolation to me. I remember thinking ' At last, I have returned home, my God this is my home.[5]

I did see a bright orb that reminded me of the sun, but this beautiful white light seemed to radiate from every direction. Somehow, I knew within the deepest part of my soul that the light was coming from the heart of God.[6]

Then suddenly the darkness gave way and I found myself standing in front of this huge mansion. Golden, honey colored light was streaming out the windows and surrounded me, pushing back the darkness. I remember looking to my side and seeing the darkness fade like a fog, but trying to still hold on to me in a vain attempt to keep me. The golden light saturated my every cell, my very being. It also had a presence to it, but different from the darkness. It was filled with so much joy that the feeling was more real and intense than any emotion I have ever had in my best moments on earth.[7]

I was in a dark void or space like in the universe without the stars in the distance was a light no definite shape similar to a puddle of spilled water. The light was pulsating as if alive, I began to move toward the light, was being drawn, all of a sudden it was like I was moving at the speed of light.

The light was like a boundary, but it was transparent, I passed through into the light: it is hard for me to find the words to describe the feelings one encounters. I was blinded by the light unable to see anything but the light did not hurt your eyes. It was like looking into the sun a million times over a pure white light. I felt warm, safe, peaceful, and in the presence of pure unconditional love. It was like the light was absorbing me[8]

I saw a light, an extremely bright light, radiating various dominant colors of white, gold, orange, and yellow. I began to feel comfortable with the presence of the light now. It became my companion as we traveled a very vast green meadow. As we traveled further, I sensed there was a festival along the far horizon. I couldn't hear sounds. I could only sense what was happening.

I felt joy. My whole being was so peaceful. I didn't even know what pain and sorrow were anymore. I didn't have the correct adjective to describe what I felt. The light started a 'conversation' with me. It wasn't audible but I could understand the words he was saying. He was speaking to me through my mind. I can still clearly remember his words.[9]

Once I was outside, I had the feeling that it was night. A shaft of brilliant white light, similar to looking into an aircraft searchlight, pierced the dark sky above me. By contrast, the dark around me was so deep it was palpable. I 'fell' upward through that light, but when I reached a threshold, a point of no return, I was stopped. I kept looking into the light. Within it were all the love, beauty, acceptance, and bliss imaginable. How can one describe perfection? I knew God was behind that light and I wanted more than anything to join the beings that I knew were with Him. However, a voice said, 'Go back. It isn't time.'[10]

It has been over forty years since my 'death', and I have forgotten thousands of experiences. Thousands have faded and dimmed with the passing of time. Many traumatic ones have been embellished or misremembered. I had only one life and death experience that has remained clear and unchanged over time and this was it.

The moment that I entered the Light, to become one with the Light, was a moment that has no parallel in my life! It was a true experience of inexpressible love. It was a love that could never be adequately described with words. A love that could only be experienced, the ever-loving Light. I was in the Light, I was the Light, and the Light was God.[11]

At the end of this tunnel, I saw this beautiful, extremely attractive light, and to which I came closer very fast. It is very hard to describe this light. The light I saw does not exist on Earth. I would say LIGHT AND EVEN SHADOW might (?) look like what nuclear physics can produce: light is made of small ultra-bright dots, hyper-mobiles and DENSE, energy. Colors are very, very vivid, clear, as if PURE, and each light dot that makes up the light seems to be individual, but it participates to the whole that constitutes the light, and it seems to contain the whole color prism. As for the field of view, it encompasses all.[12]

As all of these things occurred, I also felt and saw a bright light. In the light was my daughter-in-law who had passed two years before. She was waiting for me. She seemed in the light and part of the light. I felt wonderful, happy and moved into the light. I knew I was leaving my husband and family behind but wanted to go into the light.

It was happiness a thousand times over. Utopian. Angela was smiling and getting closer. I heard my name being called and did not want to answer. Q / It was soft, not smooth, not textured, it was bright to the point it was all around me, almost as I was enclosed in it. The further I went in the more I felt wrapped in it. I do not know why, when I think about it I think of roses.[13]

Next, I became aware of a VERY bright light in the upper left corner of the room. I felt myself being drawn slowly towards that light. I could still hear the chaos behind me, but I don't recall looking down or anything. I was drawn to the light. At this point, I remember realizing that I was dying, and having a 'So this is what it's like!' kind of feeling.

However, I also felt an overwhelming sense of sadness for my wife and children who would be left behind. At this point, I entered the 'light' and found that it seemed to be a tunnel leading somewhere. The light was the brightest white that I had ever seen. As I entered the tunnel, I felt an indescribable sense of warmth, love, peace. I'm not sure how to describe it. The farther I got into the tunnel, the greater the peaceful feeling became. As I approached the 'end' of the tunnel, I could see people waiting to greet me. One of them appeared to be my mother-in-law who had passed away 7 months previously.[14]

I saw a small yellow fine circle so intense that it attracted me. Also my natural curiosity made me go in to see what was behind it. My curiosity turned into desire, I wanted to go into it. But as much as I tried I wasn't able to speed up my journey. Anxious and trying to go in, I managed to penetrate slowly into this small space. It was as if it was a silk thread; soft and delicate. To lift my head and shoulders, as I believed that I would finally be able to live in the light that was within, it stopped at the middle of my body, and filled every part of my body. I became blinded and was in complete ecstasy. I breathed deeply, to fill myself completely with this amazing sensation. I didn't want, didn't need anything else. I had arrived at the end, the final destination, there wasn't any way that here could be any more love than this, I felt it, I knew it, and I enjoyed it enormously. No pleasure, feeling of peace, harmony, fullness or ecstasy could describe the sensation of being embraced by this light that filled me with this complete love. There were not sufficient words.[15]

I was in a landscape of pure, shimmering, golden-white, coruscating, and living light. It was like a conscious, loving light. There were no horizons; no up or down, no far away or close. I was in a totally different, spatial dimension. It was in a place that was utterly peaceful, still, calm, safe, loving and nurturing. It was a relief to be there. It was as if I was held by the light and the love emanating from the light. I couldn't move out of it but didn't want to either.[16]

As I got closer to the Light, I was absorbed by its brilliance and perfect love.I was in the Light! Oh my God, I was actually in the Light. I was the Light! I looked directly into the source of the Light and it appeared to me in a human-like form. It looked like a massive human silhouette that was radiating with the brightness of a thousand suns. Although I couldn't remember seeing its form before, somehow I recognized it.

The Light spoke to me: 'Andy, do not be afraid. Andy, I love you. Andy, we love you.' The Light: It actually knew me. The Light knew my name. The Light called me Andy. Surrounding the central Light form were millions and millions of other Lights welcoming me back home. I knew them all, and they knew me; we are all pieces of the same Light. I heard myself say, 'It's good to be back home.' We were all home together again. ...

There is no way to compare my consciousness when I was in the Light with my consciousness here on planet

Earth. It's like asking someone to compare the difference between the light from a thousand suns exploding at the same time and the light from a matchstick. Yes, they are both light, but beyond that, there is no comparison.

I can only say that I was in a complete state of love and knowing. The love of a billion homecomings all rolled up into one instant, and the knowing of every aspect of the complete universe, to become one with God. I had all of my earthly senses heightened a million times.[17]

I felt completely at one with the universe. It was like a great light had absorbed me. It was a light free from all suffering. The light was of peace, understanding, acceptance and complete tranquility. I describe coming back to life as being 'ripped back from the oneness.'[18]

But where am I?' I couldn't help wondering. In that sea of golden light, all that I felt was a gentle and incredible warmth and peacefulness, that which I had never experienced something so pure and divine in the physical world. There was neither an enchanting heaven nor a terrifying hell that I had grown up hearing, but only peacefulness and calmness.....

At that time I felt as if I was cradled in the womb of the universe. I was fully embraced by the sea of golden light. I was completely immersed with the universe. Through the light, I was fully embraced by the overwhelming, non-judgmental and unconditional love of the universe. Greater than anything. More beautiful than anything.I understood how much the feeling of dying resembled that of being born. Perhaps life was a circle, departing and ending at the same point.[19]

I soon found myself in a space and place unknown to me, having arrived there at a velocity I was unfamiliar with, with a force of attraction like that of metal to a magnet. I entered a place where it started to turn dark as if I was inside a cloud, and it was becoming denser and darker, and in that darkness, which became almost total, I glimpsed a tiny star or light, which, from the exact time I noticed it, attracted me without hesitation towards it, with the same breakneck speed and velocity.

At the same time, my love, or the most marvelous feeling that can be experienced, was becoming larger, the closer I got, my exultation overflowed, the light each time larger or it was emanating from someplace - I don't know. The idea is that I found myself in that light. So brilliant, so white, but without disturbing me. It was pure energy, the force, the love, the life - I was already home.

The sensations are indescribable as we are very limited in this life; over there, was an unknown world of new sensations opening up - of understanding of what, up until then, has not been understood by you, and you do love, my God, how you love.[20]

As I took my last breath, my eyes closed in death and they opened in a beautiful, radiant, white limitless light. It was crystal clear. My physical form was no longer a human form. I was a Light Body. I could tell because I could see my reflection. It was like I was looking in a mirror. I found myself pulled up through the Light at an accelerated rate of speed. It was like I was being sucked through the air by a powerful, yet gentle and loving force. It was like I was riding a cosmic elevator. I wasn't afraid, though. All I could feel was love that was so powerful that I knew I was going Home.[21]

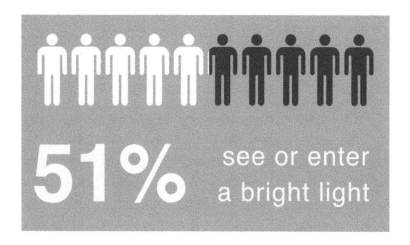

CROSSOVER RETROSPECTIVE COMPILATION[22]

OBSERVATIONS

DJK

There are two distinct types of light described in this realm once out of the tunnel: concentrated and diffused.

Concentrated light

• There is an intense light in this realm described as many times brighter than our sun, but which does not hurt the eyes. It generally appears to have a discernible location and occupies a defined space. It is often seen at the end of a tunnel, yet is just as common to be somewhere within the realm they are journeying through. It is generally described as golden, yellow, white, or a combination of the three. It is not diffused, although this light may contribute to the overall brightness of the environment.

• Near-death experiencers overwhelmingly describe the light as having a presence — a consciousness. The presence, existing within, or shrouded by the light, is often sensed to be God, Jesus, a powerful spiritual being, or an all-knowing source.

• The feelings of love and peace experienced throughout a typical NDE journey is uniform. And why not? This realm radiates similar energy throughout. However, when in the presence of this brilliant, bright light, these same feelings become overwhelming. Feelings of unconditional love, a sense of being home, and of finally understanding who they are overpower. There is a sense of joy so powerful they feel they cannot contain it. There is no pain, no fear, no sorrow, no sense of judgement, but rather an understanding that they are accepted for who they truly are. And who they truly are is much more than they ever imagined on this plain.

• NDErs are nourished by this light. They are near it, wrapped in it, held, cradled, and absorbed by it. It envelops their entire being.

Diffused light

• The overall environment is described as predominantly lit by the elements contained within it, from the grass, water, flowers, and cities to beings inhabiting this realm themselves. This might account for an environment that is always illuminated or glowing, even though it is rarely described as having a sun or a moon to reflect light. Based on color temperature, this all-pervasive light may be experienced as dawn, midday, or dusk. It is never described as "nighttime."

GS

• In the myths and beliefs of ancient civilizations, the afterlife realm is often described as containing a bright light, with deities there radiating light. Those deities often assist in the process of judgment or in the evaluation of the soul's earthly life.

• It's interesting how profoundly people are affected by the non-personal, general light that illuminates the other realm as well as the being of light they. Both seem to evoke feelings of oneness, transcendence, love, and unity, which makes me wonder if it's the same thing. Some give it some kind of "personality" and see it as a being or deity, though it might be a kind of collective, universal consciousness or group. That would explain the feelings the NDErs have – that they belong and are a part of this communal light, that their true home and unified state of being rests there.

• It's also striking how many different ways the light is described: like an aircraft searchlight, an all-pervasive light with no visible source for focal point vs a pinpoint, a small yellow circle, an orb radiating in all directions, saturating light that "had a presence to it" streaming from palace windows, "pulsating as if alive" but also a transparent boundary, having tendrils, tall beings, stars, "seems to contain the whole color prism."

PvL

• It's much more than just light. Usually, they see it as a being of light. A study was conducted in eastern Germany while it was still a communist country. Nobody described a being of light. Everybody said there was a light. Because it is an inevitable experience, you've tried to formulate words based on your own background, your own culture, your own religion. They didn't have a religion, so they said it was just a non-blinding light. Christian people will say they saw Jesus. They try to give a word to it or something, but it's beyond words. It's ineffable.

TEN

Deceased Loved Ones & Spiritual Beings

When you are born, you cry, and the world rejoices. When you die, you rejoice, and the world cries.

Buddhist Saying

I was ready to cross the threshold when I heard footsteps coming from inside the door. My hearing was so acute; I could sense every little detail. This man comes from the door. I don't think I can find the right words to describe him here. His eyes was like an endless sea of love; too bright to look at his eyes I thought. However, I started to get used to it! I know him, I thought! I KNOW HIM! I've been knowing him for a thousand years! A thousand years is nothing here, too short!

No, I've been knowing him for ten thousand years! Hmm, ten thousand means nothing here, time doesn't exist!

He smiled at me while having those thoughts, nothing is hidden here, and everything is revealed. He knew exactly what I was thinking with immense clarity and I love him, I love him so much, so much love. I couldn't take it anymore, I thought I would explode like a balloon.

He was gazing at me with this infinite love, infinite compassion and infinite peace. I clearly sensed that everything I've ever done in this life was recorded and he knew every little detail. He knows me, he loves me beyond description, and he knows I am trying to remember who he is, because I forgot, as if I am waking up from a deep dream trying to adjust to reality.[1]

There were other people running through the field with me. We exchanged glances as we ran forward. Almost all of these people were elderly but were walking like they were much younger. Some people looked quite sickly, but revived. There was one very young African American girl with braids in her hair who looked very sickly. She was the only younger person, other than myself, who looked lost.

An older lady took the girl's hand and led her forward. I felt I heard music and felt that as I moved forward that I'd be moving forward toward more people. Some other older guy had a dog run toward him. That was the only animal I saw. It seemed like they knew each other.[2]

I arrived in an explosion of glorious light into a room with insubstantial walls, standing before a man about in his 30's about 6 foot tall, reddish brown shoulder-length hair and an incredibly neat, short beard & mustache. He wore a simple white robe, light seemed to emanate from Him and I felt He had great age and wisdom. He welcomed me with great Love, Tranquility, Peace (indescribable), no words. I felt " I can sit at your feet forever and be content", which struck me as a strange thing to think/say/feel.

I became fascinated by the fabric of His robe, trying to figure out how light could be woven! .... I was led further into the room, which became a hall and there coming towards me was my Grandfather. He looked younger than I remembered and was without his harelip or cleft palate, but was undoubtedly my grandfather. We hugged, he spoke to me and welcomed me.[3]

I was now into a much larger area and surrounded by a white mist and daylight. The light I was seeing diminished all my fears of the tunnel. I heard voices of people just outside this area. The voices were encouraging me to come through the white mist. I walked through the white mist and saw about a dozen people. Instinct told me they were all man and wife. I had seen these people before but I could remember none of their names.

One man told me not to worry about not remembering any names. Soon someone came for me. The man was about twenty-seven years of age and he was wearing Levis and a white t-shirt. The other twelve people were wearing white robes. The man wearing the Levis explained to me that he was my guide. He explained to me that later I would meet other people but he wanted me to walk with him to see this new place.[4]

Off in the distance to my right was what appeared to be the shadow of a large oak tree with a large group of people standing under it. As I got closer to this group, I recognized the people standing in the front of the group. I saw my grandmother; my great uncle Glenn; my great aunt Lala; my great aunt Wanda and her husband Lee; a woman that was like a grandmother to my sister and me; and then a group of people that I thought I knew but at that time I couldn't put names to their faces.

I tried to speak to them but all they would say to me is, 'We're not waiting for you go home.' I spoke to most of these people and everyone said the same thing 'We're not waiting for you go home.' Then the last thing I remember from that side was my grandfather's voice, I did not see him I just heard his voice say, 'You're the luckiest boy I know.'[5]

Next, I saw a nice meadow with green grass that was greener then I could have ever imagined or seen. It had flowers that had a color that I cannot describe. I went inside a house and saw a young man who was sitting. As soon as he saw me, he stood up and ran to me. He looked similar to my father, but I could tell it was not him as I had seen photos of him when he was in his early twenties. This man was visually younger than I was. I asked him who he was. He told me that he was my grandfather.

Ever since I had known him, he was in a wheelchair. I was very surprised. He asked me to say hi to my grandmother, his wife. Then he asked me if I wanted to meet my deceased father. We walked for about 5 minutes. In the distance, I saw my father. When we got closer, he welcomed me with open arms. He told me that I had been a good person, but that I needed to make sure my daughter would never lose her religion.

My grandfather, father, and myself were walking along a field, and we saw a beautiful Mosque in the distance. As we got closer, I could feel my walking became more and more difficult. It felt as though I gained all this extra weight. They entered, but I could not. I could feel myself being pulled back. I heard an authoritative voice say, 'You shall not enter. You have not finished your life. When you have completed your life and continued to be a good person, you will earn your place here. I saw a light, which I believe may have been Muhammad.[6]

At that point, I saw my two dead sisters and mother. I also saw a lady I did not immediately recognize. Now, I was very close to these family members in life, and we all enjoyed a good sense of humor. All four ladies appeared to be in their 30s, even though they were older when they died. My sister Sandy was a very beautiful, slender woman in life. My sister Cindy was short, like me, but about a size 18.

My sisters immediately started joking with me about the dress in which Sandy was buried. They reminded me of a Vegas trip that we sisters had taken. Cindy borrowed a dress from Sandy without permission. She was stuffed in that dress like a sausage, and Sandy was shocked our sister was wearing it. Well, guess what, that dress is what Sandy's son chose to bury her in, and they were laughing like crazy about it. I remember Sandy laughing, saying, 'Really, it had to be THAT dress?' Cindy was saying 'I made that dress look good.'

The lady I didn't know addressed me, and I realized from her voice that it was my husband's grandmother, who I adored in life, but only knew her when she was in her 70s. She now appeared in her 30s, and was beautiful. She started telling me my husband needed me, and was shaking her finger at me to go back. I'm sad to say I argued, because no way was I going back into that mess of a body.[7]

Then I became aware of an enormous Being in front of me. I was not in my physical body but if I had of been, if I had eyes, I would have been looking up. This Being was very tall and awesomely powerful. It had a different vibration that somehow held me and kept me in one place. This Being was a light body and although there were no discernible physical features as we have here, I knew it was feminine.

Feminine is a term in this life that I don't really use, because it's not part of how I think. But this Being was, without a doubt, feminine and profoundly powerful. I was in the light looking at and awe struck by her presence, power, and awesome love.[8]

Then I heard a "thump" and I landed in this very cloudy place, and the people I saw were all dead people whom I, as a nurse, had once cared for. They welcomed me and were all smiling. They parted, and coming towards me was my father who had died six months prior. I remember how happy I was because I loved my dad so much and he had died. My father smiled at me and held my hand and led me to a tunnel.

The tunnel seemed to move slowly back and forth, and when I arrived in front of it, a bright light shone upon me and I felt no pain, and this incredible love that radiated inside of me. I walked into the tunnel and standing in the middle of the tunnel was a figure dressed in white with long hair, and his back was to me. I felt incredible love coming from this person and I just knew that if he turned and looked at me, I would be dead. Beyond this man, was an incredible place.[9]

I was immediately greeted by a group of beings, spirits, people. I'm never really sure what to call them, because those words mean different things to different people. They were so overjoyed to see me and welcome me and love me, and I knew that they had known me and loved me as long as I existed. I knew — and when I use that word know, it's a very different sense of knowing — I knew at an absolute, core level that they had been sent by God and were from God and were there to welcome me and guide me and protect me.

People have asked, "Protect you from what?" I don't know. I only know what I know. I don't know what they were protecting me from. They had physical form — head, arms, legs — and they were wearing something like robes. They were absolutely brilliant, radiating. And they were exuding this incredible love. Okay. Who were they? Was it my grandfather? My neighbor? It's funny, because I knew that I knew them, but at the time, I didn't actually look at them closely...[10]

———

In an instant, I thought 'grandma'. And I was instantly in the light. I kept saying. 'You're not dead. I am not dead. You're not dead.' She said, 'No I am not and you are not either.' My grandmother had died three years prior but at that moment I could not remember that, just that she was not dead, and that she was so alive and well (she had died of dementia complications).

She invited me to sit and have coffee like we used to all the time at her house. Her table was there, the chairs, she looked like she did when she was in her thirties. She had on a purple dress like a nice one she had with flowers on it. Except that, the flowers seemed to glow a florescent yellow. Then I noticed that there was a florescent light that emanated from the top of the room.

I started feeling so good like. 'Let's drink the coffee.' I

did. But I notice that it was not hot and had no taste. It was lukewarm; but yet there was steam coming from it like it was hot, but it was not. It's like when you are sick and there's no taste.[11]

I described them as being dressed in peasant garb very simple clothing yet beautiful colors and tremendous joy and merriman there were lots of children playing and dogs jumping and it was just a wonderful festival and it was all being fueled because up above in the velvety black skies above we're pure spiritual beings orbs of Golden light swooping and swirling in formation leaving sparkling Golden trails emanating.

These hymns chants anthems powerful like a tsunami wave crescendo after crescendo after crescendo of the most beautiful music waves washing through me and that's what was fueling this incredible joy and mirth going on in this gateway Valley as I came to call it now.

The important thing to understand is it that gateway Valley was much more real than this world. Far sharper crisper and more real than this. This is very dreamlike by comparison. That was a deep deep mystery to me for a long time trying to understand that ultra reality.[12]

I saw the Light. I travelled towards it automatically, and found myself in a beautiful field of golden grasses. I noticed about five or six people looking at me and waiting for me, and realized later that these were in fact deceased relatives from Scotland. I was shown a magnificent gold colored city where universities of learning were operating.[13]

I felt a warm light behind me and when I turned around, I was in this beautiful warm sunny garden. Everything was alive. And then I heard his voice.I saw Stephen. He had died when we were fifteen in the tenth grade just before Christmas. I had missed him so much. We had been great friends. He looked so real and so healthy now, not at all like the boy with the hollow chest filled with sawdust that I had cried over in his casket.

He had so much to show me. He was able to telepathically show me his death as he had experienced it through his eyes. First, he allowed me to see him getting out of bed and walking toward the washroom, and then falling and hitting his head on the toilet. Then I was shown how his soul had seen his head hit the toilet causing an aneurysm to burst. Then he showed me a man in white calling him towards a tunnel. This was his spirit guide.

He told me that death is a lie men tell themselves. We never truly die. You leave this earth once you've learned all you can, and then you return to the spirit world. He showed me that they could see us whenever they desire. He also emphasized that we here in the physical world have complete free will.[14]

During the time I was under for surgery I woke up. I felt myself floating in total darkness. I mean black nothingness. I had the sense of floating, movement in total blackness. However, I was not afraid. I felt very calm and content.

Out of the darkness behind me, I heard my father call to me. He passed away 10 years ago at the age of 76. I was looking toward where I heard his voice and then all of a sudden there was light everywhere. And there he was!! Smiling, and looking like I remember him when I was young. Now he was a man in his thirties and I was old.

Seeing him in this light and talking to him was so comforting. I never in my life felt so content. I had a feeling of total peace like nothing I've ever experienced. We were weightless. It was just him and myself in this magnificent light. I remember the air was so clean and I felt light as a feather. My father and I talked, we laughed, and it felt so good to see him. He was young and healthy. I remember he had his legs again! He lost both legs to diabetes before passing.

The whole experience was vivid. Then all of a sudden, he said 'Well son, I'll be seeing you.' He reached out and put his hand on my shoulder. In a flash, everything went black and I felt myself moving backwards at high speed. I remember the sound of high wind carrying me in a vacuum to a sudden stop, and then nothing.[15]

They were taking me down this incredibly beautiful path to this dome-like structure, which was exploding with color and this absolute pure love of God. I knew that was basically the point of no return. It was the entrance to heaven — whatever, however you want to describe it, that was where I was going.

When I greeted these people and was greeted by them, it was more like, "I know you, but we have plenty of time to chit-chat later. I want to get down this path." Eventually we did get to the big arched entryway, and inside I could see many, many other spirits, angels, people — I don't know what they were. They were all running around. They were all very busy, and I'm not sure what they were doing, but I knew that they were busy doing God's work.

When I arrived they looked up and had this same sense of absolute joy at my arrival. Another profound part of the experience — and again, I can't explain it using three-dimensional language: During that time, it became absolutely clear to me that these people were joyful not only at my arrival but at the arrival of every person who shows up.

More importantly, I understood how God can actually know each one of us, love each one of us as though we were the only one, and can have an incredible plan for each one of us. That's something that before this experience was difficult for me to grasp. But during this time, it became absolutely clear to me how that can be, and how all of God's promises are true.[16]

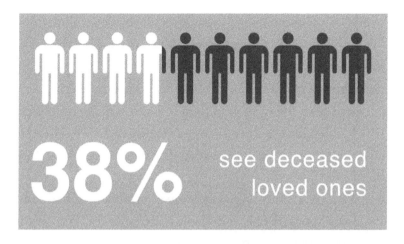

Crossover Retrospective Compilation [17]

OBSERVATIONS

DJK

• Meeting a spouse is a very rare occurrence even in the thousands of NDE's reviewed. This is surprising. With such a large percent of NDErs being advanced in age, it would be reasonable to assume that many would have been predeceased by a spouse. One exception that was found is in the testimonial of Jeffery Olsen which is described in his book *KNOWING*. He was involved in a car accident with his wife, who then appeared during a period which included Jeffery's out-of-death, near death and after-death experience. She did not come back and Jeffrey did.

Why do NDErs very often meet relatives and friends, but not a spouse? This is difficult to account for. Perhaps, if the NDEr crossed a border — the point of no return — they would see them again. It is often intimated that the NDEr has encountered their "spiritual tribe" during their journey. These are beings they have travelled many lifetimes with. That being the case, it would hold that they will encounter a spouse in a realm beyond or apart from the one NDErs encounter. We will likely never have an answer to this mystery if we do not know this by now.

• Those encountered during an NDE are described as radiant and healthy, regardless of age. Yet age is something of a mystery. There are those who look older — many of whom they know and easily recognize. Those they knew to be much older when they passed, such as grandparents, appear much younger — normally described in their 30s. They recognize these entities even if they had never seen them at this younger age. Few are described as children who appear to be the same age as when they passed, and even fewer who were children when they crossed over, now looking older.

• Why are so many of those who passed at an advanced age appearing much younger? And why do few children appear older during an NDE? Is it a choice? We have no answer, but it is a persistent pattern.

• When NDErs encounter deceased relatives or old acquaintances, they are uniformly positive experiences. The meetings are described as joyful and with someone with whom they shared a strong, and close relationship. It is never mentioned that they did not like these people or had a negative experience with them during their lifetimes.

• If an NDEr identifies beings by their sex, the male-to-female ratio is as one would expect. However, it is very uncommon that people in this realm are distinguished by, or pointed out to be, of a particular race or religion.

• Clothing worn by beings NDErs encounter is most often described as white robes, similar to those worn by the people of ancient Greece and Rome. NDErs have often described these white robes as appearing as if it was a part of the being's self — a mystical fabric or a white glow of energy connected to them. We often hear of spiritual beings surrounded by white light. Is the NDEr's interpretation of this light-energy in a form that they are more able to relate to? White robes hint at this.

• There appears to be a subtle, hierarchical structure to the beings that NDErs encounter when they cross over:

1. There are those who are similar in appearance, powers, and personalities. They are often assembled in groups. The main difference exhibited is experience — they have clearly been in this realm for some time, are more acclimated to the environment, and understand how things "work."

2. There are those who appear similar, but have a more specific purpose related to the NDEr, such as a guide or messenger who moves about alone.

3. There are what are described as spiritual beings, or angels who radiate power, wisdom, and love. They have a glowing quality, and often do not appear as having a distinctive, well-defined human form. Often the NDEr senses that they have known and been connected to them for many lifetimes, even thousands of years, but they do not physically recognize them. They may serve multiple purposes such as welcoming NDErs and guiding them through this realm, accompanying them on their life-review, and sending them back.

4. They may encounter an entity that is interpreted as God, Jesus, or a god-like figure when reported by a western experiencer. This is most often the case in *Crossover Experience* due to the overwhelming prominence of western testimonials. This will be covered later in the book.

GS

• Meeting deceased relatives is one of the most common elements of NDEs around the world and throughout history. Almost all of them have this feature and differ only by which relative met them. The beings encountered are specific to an individual's personal history.

• There are many myths of a spouse following a husband or wife to the otherworld, which is interesting in light of the fact that NDErs are rarely met by deceased spouses. Here are a few examples of these myths:

• A Native American example of being met by a spouse (which is extremely rare in present-day testimonials): in the early 1930s, an Apache Chiricahua met her two ex-husbands in the spirit world. When they started fighting over her, her relatives advised her to go back to her body.

• The Mormon pioneer Jedediah M. Grant, who died in Salt Lake City, Utah in 1856, was met by his wife in his NDE. She "was the first person that came to him. He saw many that he knew but did not have conversations with any except his wife, Caroline. She came to him, and he said that she looked beautiful and had their little child, that died on the Plains, in her arms, and said, 'Mr. Grant, here is little Margaret; you know that the wolves ate her up, but it did not hurt her; here she is all right.'"

• The well-known 1899 NDE of A.S. Wiltse also describes him meeting his wife: "I saw a number of persons sitting and standing about the body and particularly noticed two women apparently kneeling by my left side and I knew that they were weeping. I have since learned that they were my wife and my sister, but I had no conception of individuality. Wife, sister, or friend was as one to me. I did not remember any conditions of [the] relationship, at least I did not think of any. I could distinguish sex, but nothing further."

PvL

• Some people are aware of the presence of deceased friends or family members, people who they clearly recognize. Sometimes these people look healthy, even though the prevailing memory of them is as very sick and weak in the period before they died. If they died at a very young age, they may look like young adults now. Some NDErs see individuals they have never met before, or of whose death they could not have been aware. They feel a strong connection with the thoughts and feelings of people who have died in the past.[18]

• There is indeed always a kind of 'subjective' interpretation about how the deceased relatives look and which clothes they have. We cannot imagine here with a waking conscious in this physical world, how this works. You can recognize deceased relatives because of what you feel, because the essence of who they are or who they were is still there. I believe it is a kind of subjective projection. When they were very old, you can see them middle-aged. If a baby died, you can see them as a young adult. They may have changed into this kind of non-physical form. It's not a real physical form, but it is a kind of form we can recognize.

• "What is a guide? Who is it?" Usually, they don't know, but they call it an angel or a guide. It is difficult to see a difference between 'guides' and 'spiritual beings' or 'angels.' It's not a deceased relative. They look like a god or an angel, and sometimes I know stories where they said,

"When I was back in my body, I still could discuss things with this guide or angel." Young children can often see someone in their room who they call their angel, and this is perhaps the same being there. So, perhaps we all have some guardian angel who will lead us both there, as well as in this world, but we don't see it. This is speculation.

ELEVEN

The NDE Environment

NATURE, STRUCTURES AND THE UNIVERSE

Seeing death as the end of life is like seeing the horizon as the end of the ocean.

DAVID PEARLS

I was walking through a hauntingly, magical wooded area. It was an old-growth forest with trees so tall and thin that their scant canopies reached up to the heavens so it seemed. At least it was past where my conscious self could see. Their trunks were narrow, smooth, light and refreshing. Their leaves were green with just a hint of fall coloring. There were giant birch trees, but in a forest I'd never before seen or visited in real life.

It was a completely foreign world. It was quite possibly the farthest I've ever traveled, and yet I have no real way of measuring the distance. The whole scene was that part of the afternoon, close to sunset. It was not quite golden, but the color when the light is about to start fading away. The colors were otherworldly, suffusing everything in a golden glow. The light was coming from all around, yet there was no single source that I could tell. I couldn't tell you the colors of the leaves, they were so far over my head. It was as though the forest stretched upwards for forever.

What struck me the most, though, was the silence. The silence so complete, so unlike any other forest I'd ever been in my waking life. Normally, forests are almost as loud as cities with chirping birds and insects, rooting animals, the rustle of the wind in the leaves, leaves crunching underfoot, and water rushing in streams nearby. But here, the silence was anything but oppressive. It was liberating in a way. The earth was carpeted with a bed of soft leaves, somewhere between green and goldish-red in color. As though I was in the autumn of my life.[1]

The next thing I remembered was flying through a dark tunnel at a speed that felt faster than the speed of light. I could see a golden light far in the distance. Then the light got progressively closer and bigger until I was at the point of collision with it. And bang! It was like the sparks from a fire cracker. I crashed into what felt like a swimming pool filled with love instead of water.

Only Suddenly I was teleported to this gigantic hall that seem like Grand Central station in Manhattan but 100 times bigger. This place was filled with billions of people in white robes; people of all races, ethnicities, gender, and ages. There was a feeling of love that reverberated through everyone. There was also a song that played endlessly. The song was too perfect to describe.

As I was floating and enjoying the sense of love that permeates through the beautiful, gigantic hall or auditorium, a hand grabbed my hand. I couldn't see who it was, but it flew up with me, and we left this place behind. We were flying through the clouds. Then I saw the surface of the earth and a map-sized images of my island. We came closer and closer to earth until I could see the central hospital in my town. I woke up suddenly in the intensive care unit surrounded by my family and doctors.[2]

I became curious. What would happen if I continued to float up? I began to go up, up, and up. Finally, I could see the entire city of Samsun. As I started to rise, I could see the Black Sea and the Southern tip of Ukraine, which is geographically close to Samsun. Eventually, I could see all of Turkey and Ukraine. Then all of Eurasia. I kept going up so high that I was eventually able to view the whole earth from outer space.[3]

Although I felt the experience, I can best describe it in terms of vision. The grass was so green it hurt to look at it, and it felt so good! I could even taste the grass by feeling it, it tasted like watermelon. Walking on the grass was wonderful - it was an incredible feeling. The best way I can describe it was, 'OH MY GOD! WOW!!!'

The sense of smell was not with the nose. It was more like it permeated through my cheekbones under my eye, like smelling through the sinuses. ....Then three yellow lights came forth. They came from the left side of an unbelievably intensely colored green pine tree (color of maple leaf in summer time with light coming through it). I got the feeling of yellow and the taste of lemonade. Not yellow like a banana, but it was more the emotion and feeling of yellow[4]

When I exited the other end of the tunnel, I was standing in a grassy field that had low gently rolling hills. There were a few large oak trees and flowering bushes. I realized I was standing on a narrow sandy path and started walking along it. I didn't know where I was going but felt compelled to follow it. It felt like I was home and had lived there for a very long time.

The path lead over a slow rolling hill and when I got to the top, I could see the path lead to a small white bridge that crossed a small creek in the valley. I wish I could describe the vividness of the colors of the grass, flowers, sky, even the clarity of the water in the creek. It was like crystal. This is why I don't tell very many people. They can't comprehend and I can't explain. I followed the path toward the bridge. It was a wooden arch bridge about ten feet long and four or five feet wide. It had a wooden handrail on each side.[5]

Then suddenly the darkness gave way and I found myself standing in front of this huge mansion. Golden, honey colored light was streaming out the windows and surrounded me, pushing back the darkness. I remember looking to my side and seeing the darkness fade like a fog, but trying to still hold on to me in a vain attempt to keep me.

The golden light saturated my every cell, my very being. It also had a presence to it, but different from the darkness. It was filled with so much joy that the feeling was more real and intense than any emotion I have ever had in my best moments on earth.

In the front part of the mansion, the exterior of which extended further than my peripheral vision allowed, I saw a massive oak door and it swung open. At first, my eyes were overpowered by the brilliance inside, but after a brief moment I was able to see this large hall filled with people, all dressed in white. The place sparkled. There was a golden staircase at the rear of this hall leading to other sections. It had a very festive mood.[6]

The colors were interactive and alive. It seemed like a paradise, except the colors were alive and the rocks and sky and grass and water all seemed to be so very beautiful and they seem to all interact with each other.[7]

It seemed to me that I was high up in space. Far below I saw the globe of the Earth, bathed in a gloriously blue light. I saw the deep blue sea and the continents. Far below my feet lay Ceylon, and in the distance ahead of me the subcontinent of India. My field of vision did not include the whole Earth, but its global shape was plainly distinguishable and its outlines shone with a silvery gleam through that wonderful blue light.

In many places the globe seemed colored, or spotted dark green like oxidized silver. Far away to the left lay a broad expanse – the reddish-yellow desert of Arabia; it was as though the silver of the Earth had there assumed a reddish-gold hue. Then came the Red Sea, and far, far back – as if in the upper left of a map – I could just make out a bit of the Mediterranean. My gaze was directed chiefly toward that.

Everything else appeared indistinct. I could also see the snow-covered Himalayas, but in that direction it was foggy or cloudy. I did not look to the right at all. I knew that I was on the point of departing from the Earth. Later I discovered how high in space one would have to be to have so extensive a view – approximately a thousand miles! The sight of the Earth from this height was the most glorious thing I had ever seen.

After contemplating it for a while, I turned around. I had been standing with my back to the Indian Ocean, as it were, and my face to the north. Then it seemed to me that I made a turn to the south. Something new entered my field of vision. A short distance away I saw in space a tremendous dark block of stone, like a meteorite. It was about the size of my house, or even bigger. It was floating in space, and I myself was floating in space.[8]

As I stood there in the garden, which was to the left of a huge glorious city, I noticed once again, how beautiful and brilliant the colors of the flowers, the trees and the grass were. The reds were redder, the pinks more pink, and yellows more yellow. They were so much more vibrant than any colors I had ever seen. The air was sweetly fragrant. It was so clean and clear. The grass felt cool to the touch, like on a beautiful spring day. There were birds singing in the trees, and I saw a stream where the water glistened like diamonds in the sun, as it flowed over the rocks.[9]

What GOD showed me that day, there are not enough word on earth to tell you, but I will do my best with want words I have. There was the most beautiful gate... We went on in. It seemed like everything was in a room, but you could see forever. You would be in one place then in a second you were somewhere else.

There was so much to see - the clearest rivers and streams. The water was crystal clear. The sky was so blue the grass so green, when you walked in the grass you didn't leave footprints. The most beautiful music you have ever heard. The flowers were the most beautiful I had ever seen. I didn't see any person who was sick, or cripple, or looked unhappy.[10]

I recall nothing of my passage through the veil, but have vivid memories of where I went. It was a place, a domain that I knew right away was a transfer station - a place where beings go when moving between realms. It was like a city of crystal structures and verdant green trees and vegetation. I went into a huge, huge beyond comprehension, perhaps dome-like structure where one would go to meet with enormous beings of light/energy/color to do the life review.

I cannot describe the feelings of awe and wonder that I was immersed in...Many beings were present in the crystal city or transfer station. Beings from all over Creation. Beings going about their own business. And there were the Great Masters of Light (whatever you want to call them), of which there were perhaps nine or twelve, with whom we experienced the life review.[11]

The next thing I knew, and it was like a twinkling of an eye, I was standing in a field where the person who was with me was right next to me but I couldn't see him and I looked over to the left and there were some great big tall trees and I remember they were the most unusual looking trees. They had a long trunk with the leaves up on top, and there were lots of 'em. And then to the right of that, which would be still to the left of me, was wild flowers - beautiful wildflowers, and they were up about to my waist. I just remember looking and seeing how beautiful the flowers were because of something that I really enjoy is yard work and gardening and I just remember the vivid colors. To the right was tall grass that came up probably to about my waist I and I was just standing there.[12]

I found myself climbing up a beautiful, green grassy hill under a brilliant golden blue sky that opened onto an ancient village. The village had hundreds to thousands of people doing different jobs like teaching, caring for animals, caring for children, preaching, cleaning and many other common jobs.[13]

I heard the most gloriously beautiful heavenly chorus. I say 'Heavenly', because Nothing I'd ever heard, nor have ever heard since, sounded as wonderful!!! The voices, which I readily assumed to be angelic, sang tremendously beautiful hymns, which were replete with 'Hallelujahs', and 'Glorias'. I cannot remember any of the other words, but all of a sudden, I found myself singing along with them, as if I'd known these songs and had sung them before!!![14]

It felt like I was sucked out of my body like a vacuum. My spirit soared out of the hospital and into the universe. I mean, it felt like "Star Trek"! My spirit was traveling very fast, and I saw the earth below me and I seemed to be amidst the stars.[15]

Suddenly, my vision was back and in full HD color. I can't describe the colors because I've never seen them before. I was somewhere else, completely unearthly. It was so incredible that I really struggle to put it into words. I've told a few people this over the years, and they always sound skeptical.

I've tried drawing this place on paper because I remember exactly what it looked like, even 16 years later. I have searched for it on Google and other places where people talk about NDE, and I've never found anyone who saw anything very similar. For years, I've painted it over and over again, trying to recreate exactly what I saw.

The best I can describe it is two giant skies or atmospheres, split into two halves, like a split screen image with one sky on my left and the other on my right with a line down the middle separating them. Both sides were full of color. It scene was very galaxy-like and spacey. The left had bright, sunny colors like yellow, light blue, white, and soft wispy cloud-like things everywhere. The right had darker colors, but not in a bad way.

They were like deep sunset colors of red, gold, burnt orange, dark purple and black. Almost like a dawn on the left and dusk on the right. And in the middle of the right side was a tall thin white structure like a column or pedestal that went so high I couldn't see the top. I never detected other people or Beings there with me. I was alone, with the urge to go forward. But I couldn't go forward. In fact, it was more like I was at the entrance to this place just watching and looking at it. I wasn't in a body, but was just floating or suspended.[16]

I remember floating in the corner of the room above the operating table looking down at myself wondering what was going on. Then all of a sudden I was pulled through this tunnel to a white light where I found myself standing on this golden brick road leading up to some kind of building that had twelve pillars along the side and front with steps leading up to a personage seated on a throne.

This person got up and came down the stairs and down the road to me. All around me, I could see and feel a beautiful peace and tranquility with love and peace. I had no care in the world. Also as far as the eye could see to my left was a beautiful landscape of tulips of every color imaginable. To my right was a wall of a beautiful blue that matched the sky. I could not see beyond these barriers.[17]

My first sensation was being in an environment I didn't recognize. It was a large but finite space. Not a tunnel or bright light, but rather an area the size of a 50,000 seat oval or oblong arena. I was situated midway and elevated to one side. The boundaries of this area had a colorful, cloud-like appearance, similar to nebula in Hubble photos.

The colors were primarily deep red, orange-yellow, and set against a dark black background. It was brighter at one end of the space than the other was, but not extremely bright in any area. I had the sense that there was something beyond these boundaries, but obscured by the nebulous cloud-like walls. I almost immediately began processing the conditions analytically.[18]

There was an old stonewall, at the edge of the garden between the city and me. The wall looked like it was made of fieldstone, stacked one on top of the other, with pink roses growing up and over the wall. Although I didn't go into the city, I could see a few distant details, including a large building with a golden dome.[19]

I was enveloped in darkness, like all dark, cave dark, and I was still me but in an empty space all dark and I started to fall through a bazillion million miles of dark to this light that was a spark, the amount of energy it takes to create a thought. A minuscule amount of energy the light of a synapse, the light created from the electrical impulse of your thought.

When I hit this light, I was shot backwards and from this energy source, the universe was created right in front of my eyes. I saw everything that has ever happened since the beginning of the Big Bang. Like the Discovery Channel. I saw everything, the whole universe from the beginning of time. And time is something humans made up, there is no such thing as time this is all a series of events. It was like a big paisley of cosmos being formed in front of me and I had superman vision. (I told a friend what I saw and he turned me on to fractals it looked like that.)

I was hanging in the dark space and our universe was below me like a teacup saucer inside of a thirty-three gallon trash bag. I was in the bag still. I was beyond the far reaches of the universe. Beyond the universe looking at it with superman vision and I could see earth and my house and inside it and all from a bazillion, gazillion, light years past the edge of the universe. It was really amazing.[20]

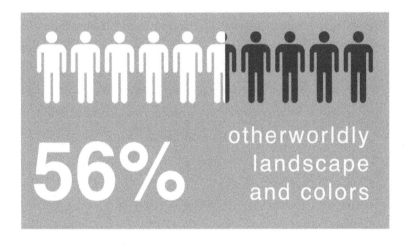

CROSSOVER RETROSPECTIVE COMPILATION[21]

OBSERVATIONS

DJK

• While all of nature contained in this realm is described as being infused with mystical qualities, the most common of elements, grass, is one of the first that captures the NDEr's attention. Many are deeply moved when experiencing grass for the first time. It clearly has much more significance than the grass we are familiar with. How can something we consider an ordinary landscaping element be experienced so differently?

Grass, even in park-like settings in this realm, is never described as having been cut, manicured, or disturbed in any way — something that is obsessed over in much of western culture. Here we cut it short, fertilize it to make it greener, and spray it with chemicals to kill off pests. In that realm, grass grows undisturbed into its natural state. Yet it is seen and experienced as "perfect." Every blade radiates and resonates energy, generating a visible glow and an audible pitch. It has been described as singing. Why is our definition of perfect there so different from our definition here?

It is expressed by NDErs over and over that all things on the other side are interconnected energetically, telepathically, and spiritually through space and time. There is a natural balance — a perfect harmony — that is manifest throughout this realm in ways we are not equipped to fully understand. However, what becomes clear is that every element, down to the very youngest blade of grass in a park or open field, plays a vital role in its great symphony.

And so grass, in a strange and deeply metaphorical sense, appears to be an ambassador of sorts for heaven — often the first way for this realm to communicate to its visitors that nothing is quite the same here. Everything is cherished.

• Water is described as crystal clear and radiating energy. It is normally flowing, as in a stream through a park or meadow, or from a rise in a city setting. Lakes are rarely seen, while beach settings were not recorded in any of the testimonials studied, although this may have been encountered. Water, very often, is the border that cannot be crossed.

• Surprisingly, there were no recordings of NDErs encountering pets of any kind in the testimonials that passed the screener, nor did they appear to search for them. One NDEr commented that they encountered a boy running with a dog that "appeared to be a pet."

• The animals that are occasionally encountered are most often horses or cows wandering in fields. Birds are rarely mentioned, and insects such as bees buzzing in the gardens are not reported.

• There is much less data on cities and towns, although cities are described more often towns. Cities are often encircled by a large stone wall, similar to what one would see surrounding a castle in Europe. A village border will take the form of a low, field-stone wall. Buildings, walls, and gates may be described as solid or translucent. Smooth or rough. But in most cases, they will be glowing a golden color or be made of what appears to the NDEr as actual gold.

• Gold is the material most often and most specifically pointed out by NDErs. It may be found as part of the exterior or interior of buildings, large gates leading into cities, and within clothing worn by powerful spiritual beings, God, or god-like figures.

• The population of cities in an NDE has been estimated to be as high as in the millions. They are often described as bustling with people looking happy and engaged. That might be in a group enjoying each other's company in a natural setting, during some form of work in a city, or when studying at a library.

• When entering a city, NDErs will often encounter large structures described as Greek or Roman in style. Two buildings that are most often encountered are massive libraries and what appear to be waystations. There is a bit of mystery to each. What are these beings studying in these places of learning? They are reading books, but NDErs do not know what they contain nor appear to inquire. We do understand that it is a "book of life" that a being may be reading when they are encountered, but this is most often reported in a different, smaller structure.

And where are those beings in waystations waiting to be transferred to? NDErs do not appear to know in any detail, and normally do not inquire of anyone in the lines that are formed, or from the guide who normally is accompanying them.

• If a house is encountered, it often has particular significance to the NDEr, who will most often enter it. These structures are not described in the same detail as those in the city and are most often stand-alone. The focus of their experience is on the interaction they have with beings inside of the structure rather than with the structure itself.

• We hear much less of encounters in space. When they are described they are most often from a vantage point of a high earth orbit. For those that travel through the universe, it is clear they are outside of our solar system, but we do not know where. Interestingly, the most detailed description of space is found in the testimonial of Carl Jung which is included in this chapter.

GS

• Descriptions of other realms seen in NDEs clearly correspond to the culture and environment of the NDEr, possibly more so than any other element. They are so different that it is difficult for me to accept the notion that they are all referring to the same "place." This leads me to the conclusion that either (a) there are different types of realms for different people, depending on culture or perhaps like-mindedness, and/or (b) that the afterlife is like a shared lucid dream, with souls co-creating the environment, so there would be a lot of diversity, or (c) the other realm is given actual perceivable form by a person's mind. It objectively exists, but the soul's mind overlays it with features familiar and comprehensible to them, which is what enables them to actually experience it. This might be the same with other elements of NDEs, and corresponds to the idea that a being of light might be the same for everyone (or at least the same type of being), but is perceived as the Buddha, Mohammed, Jesus, etc. So, the other world could be just as real as the being of light, but one person will perceive it as a lush village with fine grass huts, and another as a European city.

• On a related note, I don't see why the afterlife, or NDEs in general for that matter, need to be "the same" for them to be real. Our experiences on Earth are widely diverse, as are environments around the world. Why should we expect everyone to have the same kind of afterlife experience?

• It is worth noting that people in non-western societies *never* report traditionally western features like Greek or Roman architecture, libraries, centers for learning or personal development, etc. Instead of large cities, people in small-scale indigenous societies will describe small villages.

• On the other hand, this means that what they do share is the concept that the other realm is an idealized mirror-image of Earth. It's just that those ideals will vary. I would say that it is a general feature of most NDEs (with some exceptions, such as those that remain on Earth or in space, and negative ones), and it is common in afterlife beliefs pretty much everywhere.

• References to natural beauty are common, so that's an ideal that people share in common. Grass, flowers, trees, water (including life-giving waters), etc. (no special focus or unusual descriptions of grass, though). Same with the otherworld being a place of beauty and where we will feel happy, satisfied, not want for anything, and even have god-like powers (telepathy, traveling by thought, etc.).

• There are many references to game animals in indigenous NDEs — the "happy hunting grounds." That is more about being sustained and well-fed in the other world than about the animals themselves. In the NDE of a Hopi man named Don Talayesva, he was told by a member of his people, Warrior Society, "You think that people, dogs, burros, and other animals just die and that's all there is to it. Come with us. We shall teach you a lesson on life."

They don't actually refer to animals again, though the meaning is clearly that animals don't just die. In a Maori NDE-like legend, there's a reference to "the path of dog spirits." Dogs are common in afterlife journey myths and beliefs, either as guardians or guides. In a 1930s NDE from the Miami people of Indiana, a man came upon a giant dog, which would devour those who had been cruel to animals. In an unusual NDE from 1913, an old Ojibwe woman with smallpox was accompanied on her journey to the spirit world by a woman with a dog. It included encountering a pair of oxen-breathing fire, and a village of invisible dogs.

• In many indigenous societies, the otherworld is not just Earth-like, but an actual earthly location — often a mountain top, a volcano, a forest, a cave, undersea, etc.

PvL

• NDErs will tell you about landscapes, buildings, diamond cities, golden cities, and the libraries where everything is to be discovered.

• The colors NDErs experience you cannot find here.

The music you hear there is different from here. I know people have been looking for these colors or for this music their whole life after their NDE, though to no avail. It is not from this world. That is the essence of it. It's much more than what we see on planet Earth, in this physical realm.

TWELVE

The Five (+) Senses

OR ONLY ONE?

Die happily and look forward to taking up a new and better form.
Like the sun, only when you set in the west can you rise in the east.

JELALUDDIN RUMI

I was whole and totally safe. Everything was sharper and I could focus on it when I wanted to. Colors were clearer and vibrant. My field of view was all around. It was so beautiful and all the colors were unearthly beautiful. I was so happy and calm during all of my near death experience. I have hearing loss in my life, I did not have that in death, and I could hear much better than ever in my life. I had no trouble with my hearing; the sounds were beautiful and melodic.

The conversations I had with others did not take place with sound, but rather with telepathy. I was completely filled with emotions, such as great joy, deep, deep love, comfort, gratitude, freedom, 'EVERYTHING is as it should be' feeling. All is well feeling.[1]

I recall entering the afterlife - paradise - instantly as if surfacing from a pool of water. The images became clearer until I was literally at this garden spot about fifteen yards from the group of women talking. I did not recall any feeling of wind, a sun or any other upper atmosphere or planets. It was daylight, pleasant, colorful, but no weather, sunlight or water other than the fountain at which the women gathered. It was a very pretty place. I experienced it all as if looking through my eyes and did not have a body or spiritual form that I could detect.[2]

I then realized all the other details had stopped coming and I was fully engaged in the most astounding musical consciousness I had ever experienced. Music was not only something to hear, but to feel, to taste, to smell and to see. Thinking about it later, I realized 'I' didn't 'hear' any of the music through my ears; and yet, there was an impression of music filling my hearing senses and it included a whole body sensation. Although, in this reality, I did not have a body; so what I experienced was the sensation of music filling EVERYTHING without the limits of my individual perspective.

The indescribable music caused me to experience visual

riots of color, like no colors I had ever perceived in ordinary reality. I still cannot describe either phenomenon adequately to others. I felt the presence of knowledge and wisdom about the music and the colors, but never actually perceived being taught anything specifically.

My vision is tricky at times. My eyesight didn't change, but the way I see everything changed dramatically. Someone explained it as 'synesthesia.' I have read about that condition, but what I see is so much less cerebral than synesthesia. It is more like feeling the life essence of everything I see, including individual words, colors, sounds.[3]

Since I have had vision only out of my left eye since birth, I never experienced true binocular vision on Earth. But in the Light I not only had perfect vision from both eyes, but there was no pain or discomfort looking into the Light brighter than that of a thousand suns. That truly amazed me![4]

High definition doesn't even begin to describe the clarity in which I was able to see. I had PRK surgery done on both eyes. PRK is the predecessor to LASIK. Due to damage from small pieces of steel being drilled out of my eyes, my eyes could not be corrected back to 20/20. Yet I saw as if I had ultra 4k definition vision. The highest tech 4k ultra HD TV can't hold a candle to the way I was able to see there.[5]

I was captivated by how the cognitive experiences of our body differed from that of the soul. Whilst our body is connected to the surrounding world through the five senses, our body relies on sensory cell to detect the outside stimuli, and make the mapping to a particular group of regions within the brain where the signals were received and interpreted, such as images and smell.

In contrast, the soul does not require sensory cell to connect to the universe at all. Instead, it works in a way similar to telepathy. In that different state, my vision and hearing actually followed my changing mind. In other words, I saw and heard what I thought about. I was in active rather than passive cognitive processes. My perceptions were no longer restricted by any physical object or distance, because in that state I comprehended things through its basic forms similar to energy. That was a brand new cognitive experience to me.

At the same time, I no longer relied on sound, technically the vibration of air molecules, to communicate there. Instead, communication worked through an ultra-sensory channel. It's a pure and direct communication through thoughts, functioning through a telepathic mechanism. If we compare this communication process with that of our physical body, the latter requires constant coding and decoding and which is prone to misinterpretation and misunderstanding. The ultra-sense communication is far more instant, direct, and effective.[6]

Continuing to ascend towards the light the next thing was the beautiful stringed music. Nothing like it on earth. Also, I was aware of beautiful colors and that color has sound and coordinates with music. And the light became more brilliant surrounding me, and I was breathing it in, not with lungs but it seemed like osmosis, through every pore in my being. Each taking in of the light made me feel more and more exhilarated, full of healthy energy and brightness. Along with this, I had gained universal knowledge of all things.[7]

The room in which the event happened was completely unlit, yet I was able to see as if the lights were on. Everything I observed seemed very sharp and focused even though in my body I have exceptional eyesight (20/10 in both eyes around the time of the event, currently my vision is 20/15 left, 20/10 right). I did not see auras or transparency in objects. Depth perception seemed very acute.[8]

The first and foremost factor was the absence of physical sensation. That was perhaps the most liberating element. I wasn't cold, hot, tired, hungry or thirsty, and there was a complete absence of discomfort of any kind. I'm inclined to think that the nirvana of blissful love people feel is at least dramatically enhanced by the stunning lack of human discomfort. I then attempted to look at myself, but could not see arms or legs. This led me to wonder how I was able to experience a field of view. I'm out of body, so to speak, yet I had vision of my surroundings.[9]

I also experienced an existence without the burdens of an Earthly body. The senses that replaced sight sound and smell felt like one sense of all inclusive awareness. There was no need for physical interaction as all levels of experience were not felt or spoken, but simply known. The function of sight did not exist, as I had known while in my body.[10]

I was floating up with hand out towards this very bright light. The light was extremely bright, but I could stare and look directly at it. There was a cool breeze blowing across my face it was the most comforting feeling I had or have ever felt. I could see a great figure and was slowly floating up wards towards it, or him, and then I was back as quickly as I was taken.[11]

The sound of that music I cannot possibly describe with words because it simply cannot be heard with that clarity in this world! It was breath taking! It was so beautiful. I was ready to explode from joy! I could see both worlds at first. Although the physical one resembled a black and white movie in comparison with the world in front of me!

The colors were out of this world; so deep, so luminous, so beautiful!....My perception increased on levels I didn't think existed on a conscious level, although always knew them on a deeper level, locked inside of me! HOME! That was HOME! That's the word that rang in my ears so loud and so clear! I'm outside time I thought. Time doesn't exist! I was ready to cross the threshold when I heard footsteps coming from inside the door. My hearing was so acute; I could sense every little detail.[12]

The silence that surprised me the most though was the silence of my thoughts. Normally, my mind is anxious; rushing along in a whirlwind of thoughts that constantly compete with each other for my attention. In my waking reality, I have layers of thought, such as a song I have stuck in my head on one layer, a daydream of the future on another layer, a reality of the present pulling my top-of-mind attention.

But here, all thoughts melted away into complete still-ness. It was like a pool of water without ripples. Total calm. Total oneness. Total peace. I was completely and utterly at peace. I was one with everything. I had no scattered thoughts and no concern about my destination. I was just walking on the path, completely undistracted.[13]

It was very peculiar that it was as if I did not have a physical body. I was extraordinarily light and my legs in the grass did not touch a single blade. I was pretty confused by that because as an atheist and a person when I confront something scientifically unexplainable, I am reluctant to believe it.[14]

I saw how beautiful and brilliant the colors of the flowers, the trees and the grass were. The reds were redder, the pinks more pink, and yellows more yellow. They were so much more vibrant than any colors I had ever seen. I noticed everything had its own pitch or sound. The trees had a sound, the leaves on the trees had their own sound, the grass had a sound, the rocks had their own sound, the water had yet another sound, and so on; and, when you take all of those individual sounds and put them all together, it sounded like the most magnificent symphony and choir ever created.[15]

The next thing I knew, I was looking at someone's body. Then I realized it was me, but had no real feeling of 'Oh! That's me!' I didn't care. It was an empty vessel. Big whoop. But I noticed I didn't need my glasses and that I no longer seemed to have Tourette's Syndrome.[16]

I became aware of my senses at that moment, how much more detailed everything seemed, how it all appeared more focused, and sharper. It was like I was seeing the world for the first time with my own true eyes. It was the equivalent of taking off a pair of foggy ski-goggles or glasses. The colors seemed flat and muted but considering the lights were off in my normally pitch-black room I was astonished to be seeing everything with such clarity.

I also recall hearing cars on the main road a good half mile from my house and hearing the television upstairs on the other end of the house. I could hear my father and grandfather speaking as if I were in the same room. This was abnormal in that my room was below ground in the basement and when I shut my door, the room was so quiet all I could normally hear was my own breathing.

Likewise, there were no windows and the room was completely dark. I felt as though I had been liberated from my body and being outside my body freed me from the limitations imposed by a physical existence. My mind felt cleared and my thoughts seemed quick and decisive. I felt a great sense of freedom and was quite content to be rid of my body. I felt a connection with everything around me in a way that I cannot describe. I felt as if I was thinking faster or that time had slowed down considerably.[17]

I realized that I had the power to see everything in front, behind, up and down or everywhere at once. Without worrying where I would turn, and without needing to turn the head, my eyes could see as if in three dimensions. I didn't feel worry or anxiety. It was a lot of information at once, and all of it was assimilated and fascinated me. I felt that there had been magic in this place.[18]

What I saw was truly beyond description. Everything seemed physical in that the people I saw did have head, arms, legs. They had these robes on that seemed to be woven together with fibers of love. And I know that doesn't really make sense. But that's what it was.

When I saw the colors, it's as though I understood them. I saw them, I could taste them, I could hear them. I understood their very essence. And I realize none of this makes sense in our language, but that's what it was. We were communicating in a very pure sense. It was almost like a blast of energy. And I suppose I would say that I understood it in English because that's my native tongue. And when I think about what I was told, I think about it in English. But at the same time, the communication was on a much more pure basis.

And we traveled up this path, and the path seemed solid in that it was directional and we were moving along it. But the edges just sort of faded into nothingness. And I would say the same thing below and above, nothing existed except for us, and except for where we were going. I didn't ever feel any sense of gravity. I felt like I was a physical entity in that I had some structure or shape, but I didn't feel gravity. I didn't feel weight.

When we came to the structure it seemed like there were blocks or bricks. And again, it seemed like they were woven together with love. I never leaned against them so I don't know how solid they felt.[19]

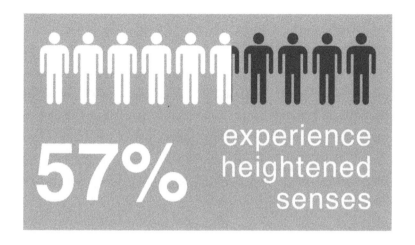

Crossover Retrospective Compilation[20]

OBSERVATIONS

DJK

• On this plain, we have five primary senses, each with its own way of experiencing and interpreting the world around us. When NDErs cross over, they do not utilize five independent senses as we understand them.

• Two senses they do consistently describe are sight and sound. Their vision is much sharper. They can see clearly at immense distances, with some reporting a 360-degree field of vision. Sounds are much crisper, with communication — the main source of sound — being telepathic. These qualities are experienced in cases where NDErs have impaired eyesight and hearing, even for those who are blind or deaf.

• Four of the five senses are not often used or experienced in an NDE as we understand them. It is uncommon to hear someone describe what it feels like when running their hand along the tunnel wall or dipping a toe into a rambling stream. We do not hear what a fully ripened fruit, pulled from a tree, tastes like. While NDErs report communication through telepathy, they do not often describe hearing background sounds, like bells ringing in the city or birds chirping overhead. And, while we occasionally hear them describe scent, such as flowers from a garden, this sense is not expressed as often as one might expect when considering the range of environments they find themselves in, or the varied elements they encounter.

• Vision - Hearing - Touch - Taste - Smell. It is not that NDErs don't experience them. It appears what they have difficulty articulating is that these senses appear to have merged. This would explain why they struggle to describe how they can taste a scent, experience color from sound, or feel all senses at once through touch. On this plain, we call this phenomenon synesthesia, a neurological condition in which information meant to stimulate one of our senses stimulates several. When they cross over, NDErs experience this phenomenon turbocharged.

• What could explain this phenomenon along with the more heightened sense of vision and hearing? This would only seem possible if these senses bypassed the physical body altogether. Their eyes, ears, sense of touch, taste, and smell do not appear to be filtered through the handicap of a physical body. We see clear hints of this as many NDErs report not seeing their physical body while in this realm. Perhaps this also explains why hunger and thirst are rarely reported. Even when an NDEr sees fruit on a tree, or crystal-clear water, we do not hear of them showing an interest in experiencing their taste, quenching their thirst, or satisfying their hunger.

• Building on this dynamic, it is rare for NDErs to describe feeling gravity. For example, we do not hear of the weight of their bodies on their legs when they see or sense they are walking. Most describe the feeling of being drawn, attracted, or pushed towards a destination. While they may be going in the direction they want, they do not often express that they are actually initiating the movement, except when moving through the power of thought. Perhaps this is how they are always moving but are not consciously aware of it.

GS

• It is interesting that Raymond Moody highlighted a crashing or buzzing as the main auditory effect in NDEs. Music seems to be much more common. I think the crashing is probably an effect of losing consciousness, such as what happened to me after I fainted from blood loss a number of years ago. It's interesting, too, that nobody in near-death studies talks about crashing/buzzing anymore.

• Some of these descriptions remind me of lucid dreams. People often say they're more real than real, heightened awareness, clarity, colors, etc. Tibetan Buddhists think it is a similar state of consciousness, and the practice of "dream yoga" is essentially lucid dreaming – intended to prepare people for the afterlife state.

• It is the case, with the historical and cross-cultural examples, that hearing and seeing are the two main senses that continue to be experienced in the other realm.

• In the indigenous societies, there were often beliefs that if you taste or eat anything in the afterlife, you have to stay there forever, and that motif features in a few NDEs. This is very clearly a cultural quality that is quite possibly elaborated in the telling. This also applies to the theme that the souls of NDErs smell bad to spirits in the otherworld.

• Sensations of movement are fairly common, especially in relation to OBEs. In a negative NDE from the 1920s, an African Tswana woman "felt a flame of fire burning in her breast and causing her such distress as she had never experienced on earth."

• In the NDE of a Deg Hit'an Native American woman from 1887, "When given food she felt nauseated and could not eat and grew weak with hunger as the days passed. "

PvL

• Experiencing 'senses' without the use of sense-organs are described because NDErs have left their body behind. How can they 'see' — perceive colors, landscapes, people, or beings, hear music, smell and feel — without a body?

• Communication is not by sound, but by direct thought transfer. It is an 'all-inclusive awareness.' The question for science is of course: how is it possible to experience all of these senses directly in one's consciousness without using sense-organs? If we don't need to have sense-organs to experience those senses, what function is left for sense-organs, or for the brain for that matter? Are they really necessary?

THIRTEEN

The Life Review

A TWO WAY MIRROR

The only thing that burns in hell is the part of you that won't let go of your life: your memories, your attachments. They burn them all away, but they're not punishing you, they're freeing your soul.

MEISTER ECKHART

Looking above and below me, I witnessed the presence of other Beings who looked just like me. Some were vibrating at higher vibrations, and some at lower ones. Yet, my attention was quickly diverted when the powerful Being enveloped me and I began to relive my entire life, one incident at a time.

In what I call the panoramic life review I watched my life from a second person point of view. As I experienced this I was myself as well as every other person with whom I had ever interacted.When the panoramic life review ended, despite the many obvious mistakes I had made in my life, I experienced no retribution – no judgment and no punishment. I was the only judge presiding over my day in court! [1]

Given time to assimilate my life in retrospect, I was given the opportunity to know, first hand, both the happiness and the sorrow I had created through my actions. I came to the realization that, more often than not, I had lived in a devastatingly selfish manner. My heart was filled with shame and remorse. The impact of that emotional avalanche remains uppermost in my mind to this very day.

However, after my time of reflection in the Heavens that day, the Being of Light telepathically conveyed these words: Who you are is the difference that God makes, and the difference is love. As the Being moved away from me I began to feel lighter. My pain and guilt lessened and I understood that I had been shown my deeds on Earth, not to harshly impugn me, but rather to lovingly instruct me.

Through the panoramic life review I had been given the knowledge of how to correct my life, and use my power of love to make a difference in the world. I was later told that human beings are powerful spiritual beings meant to create good on Earth, and that good starts with small acts of kindness.[2]

I opened my eyes, and found myself in a cinema, with thousands of screens around me. Playing on every screen were episodes of the different moments in my 30 years of life, from early childhood till the present. Some of which I remembered, some of which I had long forgotten. I was intrigued by this fascinating experience, which I had never gone through or imagined. For the first time I had a simultaneous, panoramic picture of my entire life.[3]

Suddenly, the light got very bright. It was not uncomfortable but the light bathed everything with such intensity that it shown through me. Within a moment, I was in another place with my old friend and he was showing me my life as I had lived it. The review was not unpleasant but during the review I could see how my decisions impacted others. I could gauge and feel the impact of my decisions, and how these actions affected other's lives.

There were no feelings of guilt or remorse, only the knowledge that I could have done things differently in some of the situations. There was no blame, no remorse, and no feelings of guilt. The 'life review' covered my entire earthly life in no more than a few minutes. I could see people, whom I recognized as relatives, on the other side of a river of light. I could feel their love; an intense Love is all that I could feel. I knew that there was no way that I could fail as long as I could remember this intense feeling of love.[4]

He stood beside me and directed me to look to my left, where I was replaying my life's less complimentary moments; I relived those moments and felt not only what I had done but also the hurt I had caused. Some of the things I would have never imagined could have caused pain. I was surprised that some things I may have worried about, like shoplifting a chocolate as a child, were not there whilst casual remarks which caused hurt unknown to me at the time were counted. When I became burdened with guilt I was directed to other events which gave joy to others. Though I felt unworthy, it seemed the balance was in my favor. I received great Love.[5]

Later my guide turned me over to another man and this man explained to me that I would now go through my life's review. During this review which lasted about one second or less, I saw all that I had previously seen while living on earth. I relived every conversation I had had. I saw each pet I had owned. I saw again each piece of clothing I had worn. I relived every class I had attended in school. I saw everything again. It was here in this building, looking much like a library that my life's review ended.[6]

My past flashed before me, out of my control In that overwhelming radiating loving light, I met a glowingly beautiful, very loving being. It was as if I knew him (it was apparently a he), I knew then that I knew him, and felt completely comfortable and happy. His loving presence completely surrounded me, and together we went through my life and all that I had experienced in a loving way, not any judging way.

I could see it with him; endure it all without feeling a

single negative emotion through it, which is strange to think about after. There in my near-death experience, it didn't make me wonder, almost nothing made me wonder and question during the throughout the near death experience.[7]

I did find out about the so-called 'Judgment Day' I feared so much as a child. We judge ourselves and that at first was a big relief but our life is still our job. I was shown what is now called a 'Life Review'. I was shown in living color, like on a movie certain situations, both good and bad, in my life. I was able to see and hear exactly how it was. But the kicker was as I was watching this situation unfold right before my eyes, I was forced, for the lack of a better word, to feel the other person's feelings at the time, not mine.

Beside all the life situations shown to me, I was given the capabilities to hear EVERY SINGLE SIGNIFICANT thing that has EVER affected me during my life, the good, bad, and ugly. I heard EVERYTHING at the same time with extreme clarity. I was with a Being made out of the brightest white light I have ever been able to look at without hurting my eyes. I felt it was GOD.

All the time there, we were communicating through telepathy, no spoken words. I was told 'These are your accomplishments,' or 'What have you accomplished?' (I can't remember which was said) and was sent back.[8]

Jesus took my hand and said, 'Look.' At that moment, I was shown incidents in my life where I was very mean to people or hurt people without realizing it due to self absorption or distraction. The review was so fast, in a rush, like I could see all of the incidents at once with such efficiency. It was like there was a line and then there wasn't. The way things flow there is so perfect.

When He showed me all of these things, he did not condemn me but just showed me all of the lost moments of love and how it had a domino affect on others. He was so loving in all of this conviction. I looked at Him and told Him, 'I don't want to leave. I want to stay with you.' He told me, 'I know this. If you stayed, this is what would happen to your children and husband.' I saw flashes of the consequences of my early departure from their life. In the very moment that I said that I could not do that to them, I was instantly back in my body with such a jolt.[9]

I was shown the film of my life. It went so fast that a few seconds there would be maybe be a hundred years or more here. All the pieces of the puzzle fell into place. I saw past, present and future like I was that piece of the puzzle. That is the universe.[10]

Then, in the next instant, I was suspended inside the center of an immense sphere, bigger than our high school gymnasium. The inside of the sphere looked like an enormous, unending movie screen, with hundreds of movies playing in every direction at the same time. I was completely surrounded by images of my experiences. Wherever I looked in the sphere,

I saw all the events of my lives; and I could hear, feel, touch, and smell the exact experience of living those lives. In this place there was no beginning; there was no end. I observed all of the moments of my lives all at the same time, all around me. All my lifetimes were somehow mystically connected to each other.

Strangely, I sensed no fear or judgments, no guilt or accountability, and absolutely no blame or shame. I re-experienced every thought, word, and action of each life experience whenever I focused on them. I was suspended in a world of unlimited dimensions. Then after what seemed like hours in the sphere, I was instantly back in the tunnel again.[11]

I don't remember walls but I had the feeling that it was more enclosed. I saw something similar to a three dimensional movie of my life up until that day. There was no judgment. They only showed me what was expected of me in certain situations and that perhaps I hadn't behaved the way I should have. I remember vividly that it was expected that my soul controls my body, that the body is only the vehicle necessary for life on planet earth that we are not to let the vehicle control us.[12]

I then went through a life review. It was all about my relationships with others in this review. During this, I felt what they felt in my relationship with them. I felt their love or their pain or their hurt, by things I had done or said to them. Their hurt or pain made me cringe and I found myself thinking, 'Oooh, I could have done better there.'

But most of what I felt was love, so it was not too bad. No one was judging me during this process. I felt no disapproval from anyone else, only my own reactions to it all. That feeling of unconditional love saturating me continued to be there. I was judging myself, but no one else was judging me in this review.[13]

This recounting for the deeds of one's life is not what you would think at all in terms of this life. Because what was important were the choices I made. And what was more important than the choices I made, were my motivations and my intent, and really the state of my heart in doing any single action.

I experienced in a holographic awareness that was instantaneous how every action that one takes is like a stone cast in the water. And if it's loving, that stone goes out and touches the first person that it's intended for and then it touches another person and then it touches another person because that person interacts with other people. And so on and so on. And every action has a reverberating effect on every single one of us on the face of this planet. So if I had committed a loving action, it was like love upon love upon love.

A purely loving action was the most wonderful thing that I could ever have achieved in my life. This had more meaning than to have been a Rockefeller, or President of the United States, or to have been a great scientist, and to have invented something just incredible. If I had committed a truly pure and loving action, it had reverberated throughout the stuff of every individual on the planet and I felt that action reverberating through them and through myself. And I felt this in a way that is beyond... what we can feel on this plane of existence.[14]

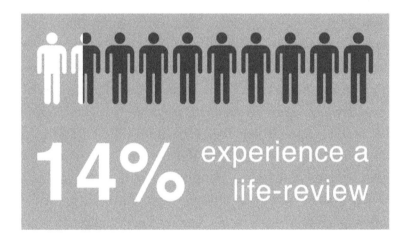

Crossover Retrospective Compilation[15]

OBSERVATIONS

DJK

• While NDErs encounter more beings resembling themselves in this realm, they are most often accompanied by a more advanced entity for their life-review such as a guide, or spiritual being. This could also be Jesus, God or a god-like figure, although this is less common.

• The life-review is a life lesson of the most powerful and instructive type. Nothing like it can be reproduced on this plane, to our detriment. This is where they experience how their actions and behavior on earth impacted the lives of those they shared their experiences with, in addition to their own. They are often surprised at actions that caused others so much pain, just as they are surprised by the importance and impact behind their small acts of kindness. It is here they learn how their actions have a ripple effect touching so many people — many of whom they never knew.

• It is often during their life review that an NDEr experiences a profound revelation. They realize that they didn't experience negative judgement, even as there were events or actions exposed that they were not proud of and were uncomfortable reliving. They did not have the impression they were there to receive punishment or atone for past sins. There was never a sense that hell awaited them, as we are often taught in organized religion. They realize they are their own harshest judge. That we create heaven and hell on earth ourselves. That we always possess the power to choose a path that leads to one or the other.

• The life-review is a most powerful experience that has the greatest influence on how the NDEr approaches life and those they are in relationship with in the future. While some NDErs may be shown the great mysteries of the universe during their stay, those are mostly forgotten upon their return. The lessons of the life-review, however, are not. Perhaps this is a clue to what is most important in the grand scheme of things.

GS

• The panoramic life review, per se, is not that common across cultures. This might be because it could come at a later stage of an NDE and pre-modern societies lack sophisticated resuscitation technology. But that's unlikely when we consider that life-reviews are pretty common in so-called "fear-death experiences" — when someone believes they're going to die, yet was never physically close to death. Examples include people who fall from heights but land largely unharmed (Albert Heim's study from the 19th century), and people who almost drown. It has also been argued that only NDErs who "die" suddenly have life-reviews. People who attempt suicide commonly do not have life-reviews.

• Allan Kellehear suggested that life-reviews are rare in indigenous societies because, unlike "historic religions," which "link death with conscience, and conscience with identity after death," in indigenous societies, individuals would not "review their past personal lives in search of sense of identity." The life-review would thus have "little private use or function." However, a sense of personal responsibility and accountability is reflected in descriptions of individual behavior determining afterlife fates, indicating the persistence of both personal identity and conscience after death.

• The idea of some kind of evaluation of earthly life is very common in cross-cultural NDEs, and some have life-review-type themes. In a 19th century account from the Tsuu T'ina Native Americans, a man encountered an official sitting at a desk writing in the "Book of Life." In the 1881 NDE of the Squaxin man named Squ-sacht-un, saw a photograph on a wall inside a house in the other realm, upon which he could somehow see "all the bad deeds of his life."

• In the Sumerian account of the death of the king Bilgames (Gilgamesh) — possibly the world's oldest NDE — he meets the afterlife deities, and during their judgment of him, they review his career, his heroic exploits, and his perpetuation of the proper religious customs and rituals.

• The idea also features in indigenous afterlife beliefs: the Maroi believed that souls must give a chronicle of their lives before crossing the river to the other side. In Africa, the Yoruba and Igbo deceased gave accounts of their lives to a deity in the other world. The Fon believed that a record of a person's good and bad deeds was kept in the other-world and used in the process of judgment. In a Fang iboga drug experience, a man saw his history being written by two spirits in the other world.

• The afterlife beliefs of Egypt also had life-review themes in the form of autobiographical funerary texts, which list positive actions and behaviors along with denials of negative ones, intended to be recited by the deceased at judgment in the afterlife. Life-reviews are also described in the ancient Vedic Indian texts.

• More recently, there are also examples of Thai, Chinese, and Indian life-reviews. In the latter, the soul is commonly read a document outlining his/her good and bad deeds, as is done by the god Citragupta in Hindu mythology.

PvL

• During a life-review, the subject feels the presence and renewed experience of not only every act but also every thought from one's past life. Everything happens at about the same moment — you experience (re-live) all aspects of your life from birth, and sometimes even before, in relationship with others.

• Because one is connected with the memories, emotions, and consciousness of another person, you experience the consequences of your own thoughts, words, and actions to that other person. And one realizes that all of it is an energy field which influences oneself as well as others. All that has been done and thought seems to be significant and stored.

• Past and future are both available at the moment you focus. Patients survey their whole life in one glance; time and space do not seem to exist during such an experience. People can talk for days about the review, even despite the cardiac arrest only taking mere minutes.

• The life-review is a learning experience, and that's it. It's all about love and helping people. It's about love, about love, about love, and about love. It's about the feeling and the knowing that you're always connected with other people, animals, and plants. It's an experience of oneness.

You not only know that it's all about love, but also that you're connected to such love.

• There is no judgment in the life-review. There is no condemnation. There is nothing that you did wrong. No, you learned from it. You failed somewhere, and nobody will say, "You were wrong." It's an intuitive realization.. Everything you do to others will come back to you as well — positive or negative aspects. And that's why they change the way they live as well. It had to be about love.

• People feel like they can see part of the life that is yet to come at this stage of the experience, too. Time and distance are no longer barriers.

FOURTEEN

In the Presence of God

Death is nothing else but going home to God, the bond of love will be unbroken for all eternity.

MOTHER TERESA

I did not experience a tunnel, but rather was enveloped in a beautiful light of love and knew I was being held on the lap of Jesus like a child. It is a feeling of unconditional love, the closest I can possibly come is the overwhelming love I felt for my tiny daughter when I held her - but even that is not the same.

I did not have a life review, but rather Jesus and I had an astounding conversation where he patiently answered all my questions. One I distinctly remember: I had recently completed a grueling course in calculus and had gotten all the final exam answers correct except one - I wanted to know the answer to that question.

Jesus laughed and then gave me the answer, not in words but in a 'knowing' that encompassed not just the element of the question, but a complete understanding of all relational aspects of the question. HE has a wonderful sense of humor and I distinctly got the feeling that HE enjoys us humans as a father enjoys watching the minor scrapes children get themselves into.[1]

I had come to my lord. In the most perfect place, and I had been accepted by my God in his house! How wonderful is that! I felt as though I had come home. From perfection to be born into sin, live in imperfection, never fully under-standing the wonder of God, and then finding yourself at his door as he welcomes you in.[2]

At the end of the tunnel was a light, which was Jesus' robe. Suddenly, I was standing in the valley of the shadow of death with a small stream of water running at my feet. On the other side, facing me was Jesus! His hands were held out to me; his face expressed love. His message to me (although His lips did not move) was 'I love you and forgive you your sins and I will wait with you until God decides whether you are to go home now or later.' I was so happy and at peace. God's will and mine were the same... In the valley of the shadow of death, mountains rose behind Jesus and a small stream of water ran directly in front of His feet; If I had crossed over the stream of water I would have been gone forever.[3]

Then my father led me into this rotating tunnel, where at the end was a very beautiful garden. In the middle of the tunnel was a figure, who had his back to me. I was immediately thrown to my knees as my father stood next to me. My immediate thoughts moved to the Old Testament, where the Levites were attending the Arc of the Covenant, where the holy of holiness resided.

I felt as if I were in this place and if the figure, who I thought was Jesus, turned around I would surely die. I heard three voices speak to me in unison. They said, 'You can stay or you can leave.' I remember when I heard this, I thought, 'I can stay or I can leave?' A part of me wanted to stay, yet another part of me wanted to leave. For I loved my father and he was next to me and I wanted to stay with him.

I replied back to the voices, 'But I am not good enough to be here.' The most beautiful voice said to me, 'Oh, but you are.' I remember I was so humbled by this that even now when I think of it I cry. I kept trying to decide what to do, but could not make a decision.[4]

With absolute humility, I uttered 7 words, 'I'm gay, will you still love me?' The Brilliant, Loving Light formed into

Wings. At GodSpeed, He whisked me into His vast spiritual arms while huddling up the Universe. I saw planets, stars, galaxies, and clusters all being brought into a Cosmic God-Hug. On a human, the place where I was taken would be the Heart. As God brought me in for a Cosmic Hug, He said, 'You are my child. I love you. I love you. I love you. Go tell 'em.' He said it with a Southern accent. He patted me on the back like a coach encouraging his player to get back in the game.[5]

I feel sorry for anyone who says there is no GOD. When I died, I entered into heaven. I couldn't take my eyes off of what I saw. Angels had me underneath each arm, one on my left and one on my right arm. I was aware of their presence, but I couldn't take my eyes off of what was in front of me.

What I saw was like flying a plane into a very rural airport. It was like when you see a light way out in front of you and it gets bigger and brighter the closer you get to it. I believe this is the light at the end of the tunnel effect we hear so much about.I saw a wall of the whitest of white clouds with a light emanating from them. I KNEW what was behind those clouds and I KNEW what the source of that light was, I KNEW it was Jesus![6]

A door opened, the kind of door that elevators have. I saw a glimpse of Heaven. This was the Garden of Eden, the way God intended it to be. It was too beautiful for words. I had that feeling you get when you see something truly amazing, breathtakingly beautiful. I miss it. Anyway, there was a figure who came from one of the mountains. He glowed like white golden light, very warm and peaceful. When he got closer, I knew he was Jesus. He still had holes in his hands. He told me I still had a job to do.[7]

Jesus walked up to me. He was tall and so beautiful! His hair was dark and wavy, and very long down to his waist. His skin was dark, his eyes were a warm liquid brown, and he had a smile that melted my heart. He told me that He loved me, that He had walked beside me every day of my life and that He had never left my side. He told me He never would leave my side, not ever. He told me not to be afraid. I just stared at Him. I couldn't speak he was so beautiful. To think He actually died for me. I was speechless, as he stood there declaring His love for me.[8]

Yes I saw Jesus Christ the Lord. He had brown hair, blue-green eyes and was wearing a flowing white and cream shirt. There were flowing grains of grass and blue sky with bright white clouds, sunflowers and animals in the background. The tone of his voice was peaceful but clear.[9]

I was in the throne room of God. Jesus Christ was seated next to God. The throne room was pure white. Then I stood there in absolute awe at the beauty of Jesus. Jesus was wearing a white robe with a purple sash and had flames in his eyes. His golden crown had many bright jewels in it. The jewels were purple, green, and red. I looked back at Jesus and his sash. Then the sash turned red. I was looking into His eyes. I saw forever in them: He was so beautiful. Then I remember bowing before Jesus and God. They both spoke to me, but I do not remember what was said by them. Then I woke up with a machine breathing for me.[10]

When I thought about that, it was like transporting by only wishing that with my mind, I arrived at the end of the stream that was very narrow. I bumped into a strong ray of light like an intense white ray. I even had to close my eyes until I was not dazzled. Before I opened my eyes, I was thinking that God was that light. While I was opening my eyes, until I could penetrate that light, what I saw was the Virgin of Guadalupe as if made of pure gold. She was shining like the light of the sun. The sparks of her layer were like light sparks. Her rays were shining intensely all around. It was pure light, really beautiful! I was standing there just looking at her for a moment until I saw her face for a moment.[11]

At that moment I looked up and saw my destination. I was looking in awe at God. It was like everything was happening at once. As I was staring up at God in amazement, every gay slur or violent act ever impressed upon me ran through me with such a flow. Events in my life played back in my mind like a movie. I felt a deep heaviness as I stared directly at an Almighty, Genderless God. I was thinking, 'Was this the Lake of Fire moment? Would I be cast into Hell for being an abomination?' [12]

While I was dead, I appeared in a huge lit up expanse. I saw both of my grandmothers. They both hugged me and my Dad's Mom took my hand and said to come on she had someone she wanted me to meet. We walked on this long golden road. It was one sheet of gold so wide you could fit a thousand people across it.

I saw a man with long white hair and robe with gold trim playing with children. He arose, marshaled the kids away, and walked towards us. When He reached us, my Grandma said, 'Honey, this is your Lord and Savior, Jesus Christ.' .. realize that I actually felt the hugs from my grandmothers and the touch of Jesus on my head. The way He talked to me was real. [13]

Everything that I perceived as existing could be experienced as the most intense light I could possibly imagine. I remember it as being a hundred times brighter than the sun, but it was not painful to experience. I had the sense that the light was responsible for everything I had been a part of since leaving my Earthly body. I don't know if I can describe this source of light as God or Jesus or any other divine being. It was far deeper than we can describe in Earthly terms or feelings.

I had an awareness of this 'source' that needed absolutely no means of conveyance or communication. I had become a part of this 'source' to the extent of oneness. Maybe I had become part of this 'source'. The thing I remember the most is how distant I had become from the physical body. When we express as humans the hope to one day be reunited with departed friends and family there is no way to explain how we will truly be together again.

The reunion is not as father and son or as our dear friend. It's as if our souls are part of an atom that had been split with all the destructive force of the universe and then suddenly come back to form a single atom again. This atom somehow contained every experience ever thought felt or imagined. Nothing ever beckoned me to the light or tried to persuade me to come or go. Our souls just know where we belong. And as fast and beautiful this transition had occurred it was over.[14]

When I got there, I saw a line of people waiting in a white room that didn't seem to have borders or lines. The light of the room was an unnatural but beautiful and comforting light. Just when I thought to myself, 'Wow there are lines even in heaven,' I was immediately sitting with my knees to my chest. I was with Jesus who was also sitting the same way. He was tall with beautiful, tan skin. His eyes were the most vibrant green-blue that I had never seen. His eyes looked like jewels. They were so full of love and I felt full of love and comfort, acceptance and utter joy. I saw myself in a glorified type of body. My hair was thick and long; my blue eyes were even more blue and my skin was flawless.[15]

I popped up into a surrounding that was white mist cloud; I saw white granite structures illuminated from the inside out. I smelled roses, honeysuckles, vanilla oranges, cinnamon, myrrh, and more all rolled into one fragrance. The flowers were surrealistic, light and bright or deep and comforting.

Then it happened. I felt a hand on my right shoulder. As I tried to turn to look, the voice was a man's voice that was soft, calming and creamy. His hand was like an aurora borealis, like in Alaska, you could see the shape but the skin was crystalline of all colors, long lanky fingers, and medium wrist. He said, 'Raven, you cannot stay this is not your time, you need to go back now.' I said, 'I just got here, who are you?' He said, 'You know who I am.' I said 'God?' He said yes.

I thought God was a woman, my heroes and warriors were all women, I believed in the sacred feminine based on my childhood. Though my mother was Catholic, my grandmother raised me and aunts separate from my siblings to be a medicine woman. He then said, 'You must leave and you must leave now.' I said I don't want to go. 'You raven have much to do, it is not over for you...Liberal ' I am now a

Christian, still practicing some shaman, WICCA, TEACHER AND MENTOR'.[16]

OBSERVATIONS

<u>DJK</u>

• God is most often described as male, and when identified by an NDEr as representing a specific religion, is most often described as the Judeo-Christian God. There is rarely mention of another God or well-known spiritual figure encountered in this realm — Allah, the Buddha, Brahman. This is likely due, in large part, to the fact that an over-whelming majority of the testimonials researched and presented in this book are from people who live in predominantly Christian, English-speaking countries: the United States, U.K, Australia, and Canada.

• NDErs, when aware they are in God's presence, often describe Him as obscured by an intense light or a white mist. While it is less common that He appears in physical form, He does interact with them directly. He always radiates great power and unconditional love.

• Jesus more often appears in human form and interacts directly with NDErs. While he is described as possessing the same qualities as above, his physical description will vary. He may be the NDER's size or extremely tall. He may be radiating light or appear as we do. His skin may be dark or light or tan. He often has beautiful hair that may be wavy, dark, brown, or even white. Often, He is wearing a white robe, and sometimes jewels or gold, as in a crown. His eyes are always described as piercing and radiating love. They're full of warmth, just like his smile.

• Spiritual beings are not often described as someone they recognize, nor do they appear as often in a clearly relatable, human form. They radiate a feeling of unconditional love and appear to be with the NDErs to guide them through varying aspects of their journey.

• Whether God, Jesus, or other god or god-like beings, it is extremely uncommon that they speak in what we might describe as "religious language." Their conversations are clear, simple, approachable and direct.

• NDErs rarely describe being frightened in their presence, although many feel an overwhelming sense of awe that may be interpreted as intimidation. Many report feeling unworthy to be in their presence and a feeling they should not look directly into their eyes. These encounters most often portray an all loving, non-judgmental, nurturing presence who displays a sense of humor and a palpable joy at being with the NDEr.

GS

• Non-Christians rarely see Jesus or the Christian god. Similarly, Christians do not usually report seeing the Buddha, Krishna, etc. It's again similar to other features of NDEs. Indigenous people in a rainforest won't see a Greek city, and New Yorkers won't see an African savanna.

• There is a famous part of the Tibetan Book of the

Dead that addresses this. It states that at death the 'Dharma-Kaya of Clear Light' (i.e. the Absolute) will be experienced in whatever form will most comfort and calm the individual. As the book's translator, Kazi Dawa-Samdup (1868–1922), clarified: "Thus, to appeal to a Shaivite devotee, the form of Shiva is assumed; to a Buddhist, the form of the Buddha Shakya Muni; to a Christian, the form of Jesus; to a Moslem, the form of the Prophet; and so on for other religious devotees; and for all manners and conditions of mankind a form appropriate to the occasion."

• So, either there is just the one deity, or "Absolute" as the Tibetans believe, and it is perceived in different ways by different individuals; or there are a number of them and they come specifically to those who believe in them.

• In essentially every religious tradition, the afterlife realm is also the realm of the gods. Spirits of the dead will meet them in the other world, dwell with them, become one of them, or even merge with them.

• The only indigenous examples I know of in which NDEs have Christian features is when they've already been converted or otherwise exposed to missionary teachings.

FIFTEEN

The Knowledge of Everything

ANSWERS BEFORE YOU CAN ASK

Of course you don't die. Nobody dies. Death doesn't exist. You only reach a new level of vision, a new realm of consciousness, a new unknown world.

HENRY MILLER

It was as if my head was opened and all the knowledge of the universe was being put in my mind with the volume and pressure of a fire hose. I understood everything. Everything. It was not 'God like' it was more of a 'cosmic consciousness' event. I could see the 'Great Spirit' (if you will) in everything. Everything is alive or is made up of this all inclusive consciousness. The dirt, rocks, the breath of a mountain goat, in the e-coli virus, the wind vapor on Mars, the varnish on my desk, the solar wind from the stars. Everything. Everything.

I am not trying to say that now I 'know' everything and you don't and now I'm better than you. That was another eye opener, now that I think of it. We are no better than the lowest microbe, we just think we are. It is our ego that hurts us. But I understand everything. It was like being tossed into an ocean of compassion.[1]

Everything seemed to be happening at once; or time stopped or lost all meaning No time, only universe; reality is in the words even: Reality = Real Light, simultaneous experience, constancy, now-ness; a harmony beyond music, purity of creation. I was experiencing being in the knowing of everything. I was aware of all and everything that is, was, and ever shall be. It was a feeling of great wonder, like a child of innocence yet ancient and fully comprehensible. I understood EVERYTHING!

It was a wondrous feeling of knowing at a level beyond 'normal' feeling or knowing, perhaps 'boundless wisdom' may describe it for you. I knew how everything came about through desire and addiction to behaviors, through yearning and fearful thoughts, through materialistic grabbing onto, and how beings/humans longed to find a way through but gave up due to constantly being magnetized to their fearful connections. Not trusting their own heartfelt truths; giving their energy to negative forces, wanting to fit in.

I knew everything about the world, animals, insects, ocean life, plants and trees, water, air, fire, the winds, the sky, song: all these things have life. The Great Mother Earth who loves us all, the harmony which waits silently in the background of all experience for those with eyes to see.[2]

Everything about the universe. Instant and ABSOLUTE knowledge. Before you could finish thinking of a question you knew the answer immediately. And it was the absolute correct answer. There were no 'well I guess this.' It was absolute truth. There was no second guessing! I KNEW.[3]

A dark haired human being stopped in front of me and introduced himself as my entrance into the records of all, everything that has ever happened, or is going to happen. The library of all existing knowledge for all of God's creatures. He shared all kinds of information with me, and even let me see other life I will be experiencing. I was given the choice to leave life on earth and continue on, or, he recommended I return to earth and complete this life cycle. He said it was important to complete each life and its teachings before going on.[4]

It seemed like it was all instantaneous. I had no limits of body or mind. I was in perfect unity with all that was around me and I was with and part of God. I passed through things that I was surprised I went through feeling like 'Wow this is cool I can go anywhere.' And space didn't hold me. I felt amazement, surprise, total peace, incredible love, and joy beyond all measure. I felt also like a student and wanted to understand all the mysteries of life, very alive and excited to learn. No mixed feeling, No doubts, none of the feelings that interfere with life on earth.[5]

I then realized I knew things, it is all so simple, people made things so difficult, it didn't have to be. What really caught my interest is knowing why we can't use all of our brain potential. Wow, what an eye opener. We have knowledge of this side with us all the in our head. But to live here and learn what we must to grow in understanding of emotional pain, physical pain, complete loneliness, complete helplessness, that part of the brain is asleep for as long as our heart is beating.

When our heart stops our complete knowledge returns. Everyone who dies sees and hears what they need for their crossover to be as calmly accepted to them as possible. Wait there is more I want to remember, then I am so cold, oh no I am back, I hurt, I want to go back. I was given CPR (I had no pulse or heartbeat). This is the hardest school I could ever go to, I am not finished, there is more I have to do, more I have to learn, and it will be harder now, knowing where I could be.[6]

Everything about the universe I began feeling as if I was attached to a giant IV bottle of knowledge. I was being fed all this knowledge, and I didn't even have the words to ask the proper questions. I felt such joy and elation; it was one 'Ah' moment after another. It all seemed so simple and so logical.

I remember at one point saying with a huge smile on my face 'Wow, is that all there is to it? That is so cool.'God, you are so awesome! We are the ones who make everything so complicated. I saw angels, and they spoke to me showing me a lake and, in the lake, they showed me future events that would take place on earth; which have, in fact, taken place.[7]

The next thing I recall was being shown the universe. I remember thinking, 'So, THAT'S how it is!' I was in awe. It was like a huge net, or chain-link fence, everything in the universe is connected. (Whenever I see pictures of what DNA composition looks like magnified, I think of what the universe looks like.) Very colorful and beautiful.

It was made known to me how important life is, all forms and that destruction of life tears a hole in the beautiful composition of the oneness of the universe and everything in it. (Murder is abhorrent to me to this day and I don't even kill a bee.) At the same time, I was being reassured in my mind that all was well with the earth and going according to how it should go. (I can't explain more on this point.) But I was struck by the simplicity of it all. While man runs around looking for complicated solutions, it is not complicated. It's very simple.[8]

While in the presence of the light, I could understand everything and I wanted nothing. I didn't really care what the secrets to the universe were or the meaning of life. The veil of communication was lifted and I was able to see only truth. In life we must decipher the truth from lies. While in the presence of the light, I was in the presence of absolute truth....While in the presence of the light everything made sense.

I feel that our suffering is the greatest of all blessings. We learn the most from that which nearly kills us. Each persons hardships are directly related to the lesson that person must learn. It is our choice whether we accept the challenge or not. Regardless of what path I choose, it seems as though I'm destined to learn these lessons. I might choose the place or even circumstances, yet the lessons still remain the same. Those lessons come differently for everyone. I feel the lessons are about LOVE, such as how to give, receive, share, spread the love.[9]

I learned that I have experienced many life times in many places and that there is no 'death'. There is no 'judgment'; there is no 'punishment', there is no 'fear.' There are only event and experiences that 'work for me' or 'don't work for me.' There are things that I want to repeat, because they give me and others joy and things that I don't want to repeat, because they don't create joy.[10]

From the world's future I was aware of the greatest hardships and problems this world has ever known. I know here the trials are going to get harder and harder for everyone. Those here and their children, grandchildren and great-grandchildren are the strongest so they can get through what is to come.

I can't remember in detail what is to be. I see friends differently. They are complaining about this or that. We are here to have the problem, experience it, learn from it, grow and go on. In relationships, you meet someone, fall in love, it becomes sour, you gave each other a lesson to be learned, you both carried out the relationship's purpose - if you stay you become unhappy, they too become unhappy, there are more relationships to experience you don't so your time here learning has not grown into the full potential it could have. Not to say some are meant to last forever, but some are just a stepping stone to something better.

If you are complaining and not finding a solution I rather break the relationship with that person, we are meant to learn and keep going. Learning what we do from day to day effects other people we do not even know or have met. Turning left instead of right. Going to a show instead of the mall, everything we do makes a ripple that changes something else.

We are very connected with each other over there, feel very close, and love one another. Here in these bodies we are disconnected to each other and very lonely that is why a baby needs a lot of touching to live it is very hard for us to be so totally isolated from each other. We need one another more than we know.[11]

I learned many things. I saw and heard many things. I felt as if there was a vast storage of information that filled me with each glance in any direction. Today, I understand what a beautiful phenomenon I experienced. Being outside of my body, traveling outside the limits of our reality's space and time was a cherished opportunity to know more about the fabric of our universe. While I was gone, the being that was with me, showed me many things. My memories of those things is still vivid and alive; everything from love, to creation, to math, to humanity, to music.[12]

I am sure about one thing: when I woke up I knew what a stupid thing I had done, and I never tried it again. NEVER COMMIT SUICIDE. YOU MUST WAIT UNTIL IT'S THE RIGHT TIME FOR YOU TO DIE. WE ARE ONLY HERE FOR A SHORT WHILE.

I'm no longer afraid of dying, although I am a little afraid of suffering. But my concern, above all, is that when I die, my loved ones down here will not be able to see me (just my body) and may think I have left them forever. If only those that I love, would believe me when I tell them that we will see each other again over there. Then I wouldn't have any fear connected with death. But, I can't tell people they have to believe what I tell them about my

NDE; because in religions there is dogma you have to believe.

There's no point in an individual trying to insist that other people believe things that they haven't seen for themselves. This is normal: they are the same as I am. Like everyone else, I only believe what I see.[13]

The economic turmoil we are now going through is one of those 'world events' that was preset. People have a choice as to how to react to these events. From what I was shown, the spiritual way is to help each other and help those in need. This is the ultimate act of love. But there is also the choice of becoming more protective and self-centered; less sharing and keeping one's own possessions as primary in one's reactions to what is there. This is a materialistic way of viewing it all as if the material world is more than the connection between all of mankind.

So what choices will the majority make? It is still to be seen. I was shown in 1981 that this time would come and that banks were paper empires, built on paper and nothing more. But, too, so are many other businesses - paper empires - built to collapse under pressure. How do people react to all of this? This is the key event and will test many. Will they reach out and take care of each other, or will they become more and more self-centered and protective of the material? There are always choices in this just to determine which choices individuals will make.[14]

Next, I scanned the perimeter, first right, then left. The space was lighter to the right, fading to a dim light as I panned left. I turned my attention back to the lighter end. At no time did I see a human like form, or any other form of being during the experience. However, toward the end of the experience, I sensed a presence originating from the lighter end of the space. It seemed to have a masculine essence, and conveyed a message to me.

I didn't hear words spoken, but just received it, and accepted it without hesitation or reservation, which is very uncharacteristic of me. The message, for lack of a better term, was 'Life isn't complicated, people make it complicated.' I remember thinking, in that moment, something to the effect of 'Duh!', and didn't give it another thought. I went back to my observations of the space, but in the next few moments, it was over as suddenly as it began.[15]

After my experience, I read about Enlightened beings who describe moments of enlightenment. That's the best description I can think of for my death experience. I had a moment of enlightenment. Everything made sense and I was at one with everything. I was completely wrapped in the glow of the universe and at one with the light. There was no longer anything to understand.[16]

———

I was shown many things, many realms, and many, many spirits of people and other beings. It was magic. This is the hardest part to communicate, as this part of the experience was wordless but filled with imagery that cannot be communicated.

I honestly feel such things are not for this world and can never properly be explained or explored in this world. Like a child hoping for the perfect Christmas present, has many images in his head but until Christmas morning, he can never be quite sure what it will be. Until it is our time, I feel that the answers we seek will never be entirely revealed, which forces us to have faith, which forces us to change.[17]

———

From what I was shown, the other side is home and Earth is just a place to test yourself. But, too, it was clear that we have more than one life on Earth. From what I could see, we come back to Earth whenever we need to test our growth under pressure, to see if we can actually live the lessons learned on the other side.

It seems there is a deep connection between the other side and our earthly existence. One thing clear was that we are ALL connected here too. It is just that our bodies' physical density dulls that knowledge.[18]

———

This is a training ground we come here to learn. Some people choose a very easy way and that's people you call silver spoons. Some people take the hard path and that would be your poor and downtrodden and they reap the best places when they go HOME. The more you learn while you are down in the gutter and stay true to yourself, the better your reward. Just like in school. The longer you stay the better the reward.

Suicide is not a sin, it is a sickness and people should not say 'commit' suicide because that infers a sin. After what I experienced and learned while I was there I found that all religions have some truth and some have some learning to do. The best way to honor God is in your heart and actions to your fellow man and family.[19]

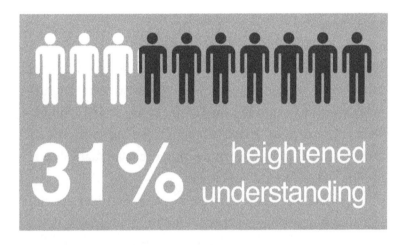

Crossover Retrospective Compilation[20]

Observations

<u>DJK</u>

• Many NDErs describe being given the answers to "everything" or the universe itself. It is most often described as if "downloaded" and assimilated in an instant — at the speed of light. If they have additional questions, they are answered before they are asked. There is often an "of course" moment, along with a sense this is knowledge they had once possessed but forgotten. The knowledge, while they remain in this realm, now seems obvious, simple, and clear.

• While NDErs know they were given and understood these "downloads" during that realm, very little of this knowledge is brought back, for reasons not fully understood.

• NDErs learn that the main purpose of our time on earth is to learn, and learn how to love both others and ourselves. When they cross over, they speak of visiting a realm where love has already been learned and permeates everything. In that realm, beings appear most focused on learning, absorbing and radiating the love that is all around them.

• The question is, if their focus is on learning, what is it they are studying in the massive libraries often encountered in cities? As many NDErs describe having learned everything in their download, what is left to learn for those who have remained on the other side?

• We are told earth is a school in which suffering is often the greatest teacher. The test is can you learn the lessons, hold on to them, and LIVE them while you are here. There does not appear to be suffering in this other realm. What then, is their greatest teacher, or test, if they are to continue to grow in love and in knowledge? This question is not asked by NDErs. If we have not learned this by now, we will likely never know.

• On occasion, an NDEr will come back with knowledge of future events. Some say they have come true, while others say they have not. We simply do not have a large enough sample size of these predictions documented prior to their occurrence to draw a reasonable conclusion as to their accuracy.

GS

• In NDEs as well as afterlife beliefs around the world, the other realm is almost always seen as a place of knowledge, wisdom, revelation, and enlightenment. In Shamanic cultures, one of the main reasons for undertaking soul-journeys to the other world was to acquire knowledge (or recuse the soul of a person in danger of dying). It may be that the libraries people see are just their visual/conceptual representations of the general concept that the afterlife is a process of learning, and a realm of the revelation of mysteries.

• In the Trobriand Islands, the afterlife realm was sometimes visited "by those who were almost dead but returned to life again." They would bring back information, songs, and sometimes precognitive knowledge of the death of a family member.

• I've often wondered the following: Could ideas about gods and angels lie in NDE encounters with deceased relatives in spirit form? Maybe that's what beings of light actually are? I don't see why there has to be some kind of separate non-human entity, especially with the idea of transcendent universal consciousness.

• The fifth testimonial stands out to me because they seem much more like they've been processed by the person who might have constructed a more understandable "story" out of the experience. Like they "clothed" it after the fact. Most of the others are much more abstract, and somehow seem more real because of it.

PvL

• I believe the brain has not a producing function, but a facilitating function, which means that it makes it possible to experience consciousness in your body, which is your waking consciousness, and this is only a small part of this enhanced consciousness. In this enhanced consciousness that NDErs experience, there is no time and space. It is a nonlocal realm. What we know from quantum physics is that everything is always connected, without time or space. There's no beginning or end to consciousness. So, this non-local consciousness, or endless consciousness, is always there and, when we are awake, we receive just a small part of this consciousness.[21]

But the brain has a transceiver function. It transcends the information from our body and from our sense organs to our consciousness. We receive information from consciousness into our body. It is a kind of interface function. You could compare it with your computer. There are one billion websites here in this room at this very moment, but you need an instrument to receive them and you can change the websites when you know the codes. The one billion websites are not produced by your computer; they are received by it.[22]

"Where are those one billion websites?" Well, they're just encoded in electromagnetic informational waves, so they're always there. They are transmitted by the speed of light. It is a kind of non-locality. You can understand it about the same time that you can receive these one billion websites in Australia, China, New York, and the United States. It's always there. It's encoded in waves. And so, the non-local consciousness is also encoded in waves. But they are scalar waves, or some similar concept. Everything is encoded in this non-local realm.[23]

When we have more reception ability, the threshold of consciousness can be lower. And it is lower when you have an NDE, which means that you not only receive channel one — your own consciousness — but you also receive channel two, three, four, and five (the consciousness of others). This is what I call the enhanced intuitive sensitivity. You receive information, not by your senses, and not by your body. It's a non-local information exchange.[24]

• When people have a near-death experience at a young age, it is not uncommon that they go on to study quantum physics, philosophy, or psychology because they remember somewhere in their unconscious about this enormous amount of information they had attained but lost. They try to find it backed by this type of study. There is somewhere, something left, but they cannot articulate it. I had wisdom and knowledge of everything from the whole universe, but I was not permitted to take it with me back in this world.

• Indigenous people have always said that you are not permitted to remember what happens in your previous life or what happens when you were there. When you cross the river, you forget everything. They may describe it as a mist, as a mountain, as a wall, or as a door. They give it a visual resemblance, but I think it's much more than this.

SIXTEEN

It is Not Your Time

YOU MUST GO BACK

We shall not cease from exploration, and the end of all our exploring will be to arrive where we started and know the place for the first time.

T.S. ELIOT

The path curved up ahead, getting lost among the trees. Somehow, I knew that if I followed that curve in the path, I would cease to be. I would 'go on' and my physical life would be over; not that I could remember my physical life in this space. I was all set to go on, I welcomed the sensation, and I didn't want to leave those woods. I loved every single second of this place. After all, walking through the woods is one of my absolute favorite things to do.

I had no comprehension of where that path led. I just know that I was so peaceful, happy, and so enveloped in the glow of the Universe that I didn't want to leave the woods. Suddenly, my spirit self felt a jerk behind my navel. I felt a tug, like a cartoon hook around my mid-section. It was a physical pull at my belly-button, yanking me away from the curve in the trees. My steps halted and I could no longer move forward. I was physically incapable of taking another step towards the bend in the trees. 'I have to go', I thought and turned away from the bend in the trees. And that's when I woke up.[1]

When I wake up later I feel such an enormous sense of loss and disappointment because I couldn't go too. I'm almost angry about it. I'm aware that for a while I 'knew everything', but can't get hold of that knowledge again in my 'waking' state.[2]

I was shown many things, many of which I was not permitted to bring back with me for some reason. I remember being told that I was dead before my time. Then I was told, 'TELL THEM! TELL THEM! TELL THEM!' three times. I was told that I was but one who would reveal the glory. Then I was told, 'Jack! You must go back. You have not finished your mission on earth.' I was not told what I was to tell them. I was not told what that mission was to be.[3]

As I got to about fifty feet from the bridge, I noticed a figure dressed in brilliant white walking on the path on the other side of the bridge coming toward me. Just as I got to the end of the bridge, the figure was about ten feet from the other end of the bridge and he stopped and looked up at me. It was my grandfather who had died in 1966.

I felt such warmth and peace and I never wanted to leave and started to go to him because I was so happy to see him again. When he turned to walk away, I stepped onto the bridge and I hit an invisible barrier and could go no further. I don't remember saying aloud the words, I was more like I just had the thought, but I told my grandfather to help me and not to leave me.

He stopped, turned, and looked at me and communicated that I couldn't come just yet - that they weren't ready for me. I had to go back and take care of my family. He just wanted me to know that when I did come back that he would be there waiting for me. [4]

I don't remember anything except a man standing next to my bed leaning against the wall with his arms folded and he showed no emotion just stared at me. I now know he was sent to watch over me. Then the next thing I know was I was standing by a gate with other spirits and looking at my hands and arms realizing I too was in spirit form.

We did not speak to one another we just waited and it was so bright and blinding but it did not hurt my eyes. I knew if I went through the gate, everything would be final and there would be no turning back. I then heard a voice of a female in my head telling me I must return that it was not my time.[5]

The way was denied me by something; they did not yet expect me, and this unique being said that I should go back and there was no other option; it was not my decision, but the most convenient, much to my regret. I began to hear other voices, to note how I closed my eyes without wanting to, and accepted what was said: 'You still have things to do with your love!' - which is the bargaining chip; it's the only thing that will let you stay there; not only that you love and that you love a lot, but also that you are loved, and loved much, as that will be the telling sign.

All your acquired liberties start fading and you start to become conscious that you have to enter once again that body, that you must return to breathing, you become conscious of who you are, all over again; you feel the voices (of the nurses). I didn't want to open my eyes. I wanted to return. I did everything to return, but once again I was in the infirmary, desolate, sick.[6]

As I was thinking all of this, I was moving fast and gaining speed moving up through the tunnel towards a brighter blue/white light. The light was so beautiful it is impossible to describe in human terms. I had the feeling I was a very long way away from the reality I had previously been existing in and going with purpose on this journey.

I wanted to keep going. That scares me a little. But I heard someone calling my name and I responded to that voice, my movement slowed down and as I turned my thoughts towards the voice my direction reversed and I moved again with incredible speed back along the tunnel to its entrance. This was not my decision. I woke up in the emergency room into a three dimensional space - disappointing. I had not had a heartbeat for forty-five seconds and I felt as though I had come back from a very long distance to awake in my body.[7]

I didn't want to leave this peace and joy but I was giving birth and feel I returned for my child. Although I have no clear memory of this decision I do recall being shown events in my past and how God was always caring for me and being told life was better than I thought it was and I didn't need to worry about anything. God would take care of me.[8]

That's what it felt like, waking up from a dream, waking up to who I truly am and this life was nothing but a dream! I just left for about five minutes of our earthly time. I found my friend resuscitating me. I was back! I am back, knowing we all live forever, joined together by this great LIFE that orchestrates all physical life to the tune of LOVE! The tune of spiritual evolution that everybody takes a part; everything that we are meant to experience we do - eventually! God bless![9]

I then went through the tunnel of black void and into the light. As I emerged into the light, I felt sunshine warmth and smelled the earth, the grasses and flowers. I came through the tunnel and standing at the edge, I saw a large green meadow and tall grasses and a body of water. On the other side stood a male being in a white gown and a black and white long haired dog.

I do not know how I got across the water but I went to them and they led me to a very, very tall golden knobbed door. As I went to put my hand on the door a being said something to me and in my mind, I started to think of my three small children. The next thing I felt was a swish and I was in total darkness.[10]

Without looking absolutely at anything, almost immediately I felt the stroke of a hand on the upper part of my head. In this moment I was flooded with an unimaginable love. I was filled with ecstasy. At this moment when the hand touched my head I heard a gentle, beautiful, almost mystical voice which said to me, 'Stay calm and go in peace. Do everything that I have asked you.' I wanted to ask, understand, investigate more but in this instant I began my journey back.

I returned seeing the layers of branches but really

quickly. There was no way to enjoy them. I wanted to but could only go back in this violent way. I didn't want to return from this beautiful experience which was so nice, and that I liked so much. Why do I have to return if I was able to rest at last? For what reason are they waking me up? Why are they bothering me? I asked myself constantly.[11]

I was ready to exit the tunnel, or I had just exited it and the light was so indescribably ethereal and wonderful I wanted to keep gravitating to it, to it's source. But I was held back by the entities very gently and told not to do that. I had the sense that it would be dangerous to go to the very source of the light, yet I was not afraid, but exhilarated. But I obeyed their caution. At that point, they told me that it wasn't my time yet and that I had to go back. I didn't want to, I begged to stay but they gently and lovingly refused me.[12]

During the OBE, I was at peace on the other side, and only thought about my kids for a second, knowing they would be okay. I was prepared to stay. But soon, a male voice told me I had to go back. It wasn't words I heard, just an understanding that I HAD TO GO BACK. I remember not wanting to leave. What for? So I could work more? Live in more pain? I was divorced, kids were grown, and felt I could easily be finished on Earth. But it was not my time, or so I was being told.

After a while, I felt the sensation of intense squeezing

again. It had a sound, too. It was higher-pitched than the exit sounds, and seemed to exert even greater pressure on all sides of my head like a vice fitted with loud speakers blasting sound into my mind with some kind of crushing on my skull. That sensation brought about the end of the celestial vocalizations and the space travel; and I quickly became aware that someone was shouting my name over and over. I felt my eyes pop open and I was face-to-face with a panic-stricken anesthesiologist a few inches from my nose yelling at me, trying to coax me back into my body.[13]

I saw a wall of the whitest of white clouds with a light emanating from them. I KNEW what was behind those clouds and I KNEW what the source of that light was, I KNEW it was Jesus! I saw Jesus riding the prettiest white horse I have ever seen. I couldn't take my eyes off of HIM. HE was riding very fast from my right to my left. We were traveling sideways and toward HIM at the same time.

We got closer and HE looked over at us, held out HIS left hand, and said 'It is not your time.'Instantly, we were traveling backwards at what seemed to be light speed. I saw my body. We were traveling through space at an amazing speed. The only way I know to explain it is like in the movies Star Wars or Star Trek when they go REALLY fast. The stars look like lines zipping past.

My first recollections are when we were in what I can only refer to as outer space, just before traveling REALLY, REALLY FAST! I remember spiraling back down through the roof of the building. It was strange. Then as I passed through the ceiling tiles and looked down..more?[14]

It was a very emotional experience. I was in the hall of my family, in the company of my ancestors back to the beginning of our line, and I was welcomed in their midst. I was given a choice of whether to stay with them or to return, and I chose to return. I have business here I must conclude, and I did not feel worthy of my ancestor company forever.

The transition back to life was absolutely terrifying. There were people running around, a near state of panic, and the crushing pain, probably from the paramedics doing chest compressions, and of course, I remember getting lit up with the defibrillator. That's a charming experience. I was somewhere between wanting to choke the medic for doing that, and begging him not to do it again. How does one describe a trip to where no-one else has been and returned?[15]

I said, 'No! No! I don't want to be here. I got here by mistake. And what about my husband, my children and my grandchildren. And my patients?' My mother rose from the table, comes over to me and takes my hand. She leads me to the corridor and says, 'It's not your time yet. We must part; you must go back.'

Then I remember that I looked just like a ghost in a comic book, looking around the operating room and seeing my own defibrillation. I saw the way a woman was lying on the bed in the surgery room. I was wondering who it is lying there. The doctor said to the assisting staff, 'Now get away.' Then he used the defibrillator on the woman. It was me. I also remember a priest giving me the last sacrament. The priest said, 'You'll go to heaven.[16]

When the person reached me, we spoke through thought. He told me that it was not my time to enter into my heavenly home but had a mission to fulfill and my life was going to be very hard. That I would go through many terrible experiences to the point of wanting to commit suicide but if I committed suicide I would not be allowed to come home. He told me that I would be watched over and protected, kept safe. If I would get through this mission, I would be allowed to return home.[17]

They told me that it was not my time but that due to a medical mistake I arrived home once again. I still had a lot do and to learn but under no circumstance did I want to return to earth. I was going through a rough time in my life and was afraid to lose all those wonderful feelings.

A being of light, even brighter and more loving, who could have been Jesus, asked them to show me part of what I still had to do on earth and to show me my new born son in the crib at the hospital. They told me that my son had a learning path depending on the fact that I would be his mother and that my decision would greatly affect his life.

With all the pain in my heart (by the way I had no physical pain) I decided to return. They would have to erase almost all of my memories because they explained that if I remembered too much I would not be able to handle the desire to return and would run the risk of committing suicide, which was considered wrong in that dimension.

When I agreed to return it was very difficult for me to decide to enter my body, so heavy, dense, encumbering. But a deal is a deal. I entered just at the time they were using the electrical metal plates to restart the heart. I heard the nurse say, 'Doctor, she has a pulse.' I then fell asleep and woke up in the recovery room. I am fifty-four years old. I am a very healthy person, mind and body. I have had dreams and nightmares, good and bad but none of these dreams have lasted more than a few days in my mind. In all of these years my experience has not faded one bit. I am anxious to return.[18]

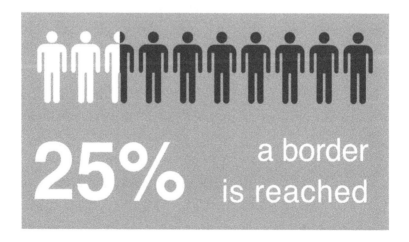

Crossover Retrospective Compilation[19]

OBSERVATIONS

DJK

• In the majority of near-death experiences, NDErs are told they must return, or simply find themselves being sent back. Fewer are given a choice to stay. When this occurs, they are generally near a defined border such as a bridge, door, gate, or archway. They are told that if they cross, they cannot return.

• What is not clear is what they are crossing into that will not allow them to return. Is it a different location within this realm? A different realm altogether? A different state of awareness? A different dimension? We do not know, and it does not appear that NDErs inquire. All they know is they cannot return if they cross over. There is no in-between.

• NDErs are often told by beings like themselves that it is not their time and that they must return in a halting, abrupt tone rather than a warmer, more comforting way. This is in contrast to a spiritual being, Jesus, God or a god-like figure, who shares the same message in a loving and compassionate way instead. Though a subtle difference, this pattern is consistent. In either case, they will oftentimes argue against returning, with some even refusing. However, once told, they are not able to remain.

• The actual return is described fairly consistently. It generally begins abruptly. They describe being pulled, jerked, or tugged from behind. They do not initiate the return or show control over any part of it. It is much faster than their entry into this realm, and often frightening. There are no stops along the way. They rarely describe what they are seeing on their return other than blurring through the tunnel.

• Reentry into their body is most often described as abrupt and uncomfortable. They may feel a sense of crashing back into their bodies or being squeezed at high pressure. Depending on the circumstances of their clinical death, they may begin to feel great pain, confusion, and extreme disappointment, sadness, or anger.

GS

• A reluctance to return is one of the most common NDE elements across cultures. It is so recurrent around the world that it should really be considered an NDE element in its own right. The few accounts that instead describe the NDEr not wanting to stay in the other realm and trying to get back are often more like legends or myths, with other kinds of idiosyncratic cultural features like plots and motifs like taboos on eating something in the otherworld or being given some kind of ritual objects or information.

• Another common description is horror and disgust at the prospect of returning to the body. There are examples from North America, Polynesia, and Melanesia. The bodiless afterlife state is clearly far preferable to the earthly embodied one. There are often graphic or emotional descriptions about how horrified and afraid they are to re-enter their bodies.

• A key difference, though, can be the reason for the return. Rather than being sent back because it is not their time, or to fulfill some earthly obligation (raising a child, caring for a sick loved one, etc.), sometimes it's a case of mistaken identity. Such accounts are known from ancient Greece and Rome, China, India, Medieval Europe, modern Guam, and Thailand.

• The method of re-entering the body is also cultural. Some are pushed, and in Hawaii, they were pushed specifically into the big toe. In a 19th century NDE from the Society Islands (Tahiti), a woman's soul returned to her body through "the least dignified of entrances."

<u>PvL</u>

• People see thick fog, a wall, a valley, a river, a bridge, or a gate. They are aware that once they cross this border, they will not be able to return to their bodies and resume their lives. Most sense they were forced to go back because they didn't want to leave. They felt they were finally home.[20]

    • At this stage, there may be some communication with a deceased relative or with a being of light. They often report they are not welcome because their time has not yet come. "It's not your time yet, you have to go back, you have some task to fulfill." The reason for this may be to care for a newborn baby or child or a relative. The way that we're told is full of love and full of compassion.

    • The return to the body is usually quite abrupt. Sometimes people feel a great force sucking them back through the tunnel. Some people describe how they were pushed back into their body via the head after seeing a nurse or doctor place the resuscitation equipment on their body. The conscious return to the body is an extremely unpleasant experience for most people.

    • Back in their sick, damaged, and aching bodies, NDErs are upset at having been denied something so beautiful. Some patients react with indignation, disappointment, or rebellion as soon as they regain consciousness.

    • After resuscitation or waking from a coma, an NDEr's attempt at talking to doctors, nursing staff, or family about their powerful experience often leads to nothing, which only adds to the disappointment. In fact, some people remain silent on the subject for 50 years or more.

    • When NDErs have the conscious return, they have a

problem because they are too extended in their consciousness to fit into this small body, which still has the problem with the disease as well. When you have a heart attack, you return to the pain. Where you have a traffic accident, or where you have a cerebral hemorrhage, there are so many limitations in your body, a stark contrast to just a few minutes ago when you were without any limitations at all.[21]

SEVENTEEN

The Hellish Realm

Hell is not punishment, it's training.

SHUNRYU SUZUKI

I was climbing a mountain which was so steep that I was climbing it on my knees and hands. There was no noise. There was a very bright light at the top of the mountain, and a very strange and frightening darkness coming up the mountain, which looked very menacing and was so dark that you could not see anything. It was a narrow and long mountain which was and felt strange. It could not exist in that shape on Earth.

I only had one thought in my mind. Climb to the top, to the light before the darkness comes. If the darkness comes and catches me up, I will not be able to come back. I felt the presence of several entities who were watching me and encouraging me. I also felt the presence of entities who were coming from the darkness trying to catch me. The nasty entities who were coming from and with the darkness were cold, noiseless, swift, fast approaching, and dangerous. I did not know why they were dangerous. I just knew it.

I knew that the nice entities could not reach me and help me but they were there. They were not afraid of the nasty entities, but they could not help. It was an extremely terrifying event. I had flashbacks of this event for years after it happened although I forgot all about it for a while.[1]

The next thing I know, I am still on my back. It first it seemed like there was nothingness, like I was on my back afloat and it was pitch dark. A very scary darkness. I remember I kept putting my hands in front of my face. I could not see them or my body but I knew that they were there.

Then I start hearing this low hum and it was like being underwater like when you are under and you can hear noise and it's muffled. That kind of thing. I was wondering why it was so dark. Nothing else mattered. I could not remember anything prior to this. Not the surgery, anything, it was as if this was the only thing I could think of.

I then noticed that while it was pitch dark it felt as if I was in a tunnel and all along the tunnel were doorways. But the whole tunnel, I could sense, was like being in a cave - sort of rocky not too rocky but kind of smooth at least that's my impression of it. So then, I am feeling a little more afraid, like what's going on here? It felt like I was like that for an hour.[2]

I realized that I had made a painless transition because you no longer feel the weight or trappings of your body. I was in total darkness that had put my panic emotion in overdrive. As I slowly began to acclimatize myself to my surroundings, I could feel evil slithering and crawling in the darkness all around me. I had only one thought going on inside me - that being that they are looking for me!

I was terrified and started looking for the light I thought was supposed to be here. I moved around as slowly and silently as possible looking for the light. I noticed it was lighter in one direction and started to move that way when I felt extreme aggression emanating from the right of me. Fearful of moving towards the light and highlighting myself with the light I instead withdrew into the darker shadow and stayed still.

As I lay there listening to the scuttling and scurrying of all the evil feelings in the darkness around me, I tried to figure out what to do next. I knew if I moved from the amount of activity that was going on around me, that I would be discovered. I was at my wits end when I said, 'God help me.' Instantly everything around me went scurrying off in every direction and that was when I felt it. It is a feeling of Perfect love and trust.[3]

I'm in a very, very dark place (frighteningly dark), but I know to look for a light, and I find one off in the distance. The light becomes a tunnel head (opening); a force pulls me into the tunnel and pulls me very rapidly through a bluish-green tunnel. I'm thinking, 'Why am I back here. What have I done wrong?' I'm slammed up against the end of the tunnel, and cannot get a breath; simultaneously my life is flowing in front of my face, no matter how I turn to get away from it.

Willing to shake hands with The Devil for a breath, I realize I'm going to have to do something about this life I'm confronting. My feeling is I'm being tortured because I can't breathe and I finally have a realization that I have to do something with this life. It dawns on me I will forgive myself for not doing it perfectly, and I say this aloud to myself. Upon saying this, the wall disappears and I'm in a warm beautiful 'really neat' place. The first thing I thought was, 'They lied to me; there's nothing to judge here with.' (Read that carefully.) The experience of being there was 'Like swimming naked at night in the Gulf of Mexico' totally supported, perfect environment.[4]

As soon as my car struck the pole, I saw nothing. Immediately, I presumed that I was dead, but soon realized that I was still conscious and this shouldn't be. I couldn't see, I couldn't smell, I couldn't feel anything and it was as if I was paralyzed but standing up at the same time.

About this time, I started thinking to myself (not aloud) that this sucked and that I was right - I knew all along there would end up being no God or afterlife and that religion was nonsense. At the very moment that I thought this, the most terrifying experience of my life began. Quietly at first, I began hearing non-worldly voices and screams of evil or laughter. I became scared and didn't know what was going on. The voices got louder and louder and soon, I could 'feel' the presence of beings or evil all around me.

The voices began to become more distinctive and some of the 'beings' were shouting 'Come with us, come with us!! Haha, haha, heehee, Are you ready for it?!' in very scary voice tones. I began to realize that it sounded as though these were demons or evil beings associated with Satan.

Even though before the experience I was very critical of religion and God, these things were convincing me other-wise and I immediately began saying 'Jesus loves me!!! The power of God will kill you all, Jesus save me!!' ...And the demons continued to yell and curse at me but at the same time they were slowly retracting from me and their presence was minimizing. At this moment a piercing white, beam of light the width of a pen shot down to us. The demons began screaming and moaning, as if they were melting and soon they disappeared.[5]

At first, I felt like I was floating in dark space. I realized soon after I was dead. I remember my mind asking 'Man, I'm dead, why am I dead and what happened to me?' Right after these questions came to my mind, the next event happened. I realized I was no longer in my physical body.

Some force like a vacuum cleaner, only hundreds of times greater, was sucking every pore from my body.

The next thing I realized was me being in complete darkness. It was like being in a refrigerator at midnight with the door closed on a moonless and starless night. I couldn't see my hand when I put it to my face. I sensed evil around me and even though I thought I could move about, I froze because of fear. I thought I was alone until I saw three demon like figures standing by my feet and talking in three different languages.

I was laying on a cold slab in a dark chamber of what I found out later to be Hell. While the demons were talking and looking down at me, there was a tiny light coming from behind them and I could see their silhouettes. They were about three to four feet high with skinny bodies, arms, and legs. The light behind them was getting bigger and closer so I quit looking at the demons and concentrated on the light.

Because of an earlier experience in my life, I knew the light to be Jesus Christ. He engulfed me in His light and took my spirit and soul out of Hell. He replaced them in my physical body in order to live again. I was a born again Christian, believing in Jesus as my Lord and savior, and was confused when I ended up in Hell instead of heaven. I think the reason God let me experience death without Him was to tell the world that Hell does exist and to spread that fact to the lost and backsliding Christians.[6]

I heard a man speaking to me, saying 'Tommy, come here!' and it was my grandfather Tom leaning against the wall.

He said, 'Tommy, don't go down there!' He pointed to the right and I saw a long, wide walkway that sloped in a downward direction. On that walkway, there were hundreds of poor people being dragged along by small men who were attacking them, biting them and beating them as they went. The smell was the worst thing that I have ever smelled. The smell of burning flesh. When I was a child I had smelled that same smell coming from a car crash site that was on fire, but this was far worse than that.[7]

***

The next thing I remember is that I found myself in the long tunnel through which I was moving forward. I wasn't walking because I didn't have the body. I began to realize that I was dying. I didn't want to die. Then I began fighting with all I had to get back to life. That's when the long battle between death and me began.

I was struggling so hard to pull onto one side, and death was pulling to another. I just didn't allow it to pull me away. I had so much strength and I was extraordinarily powerful, which totally surprised me at that point. I kept wondering where do I get all that strength from since I always had very weak hands. To me, that fight looked like pulling a rope with a flag in the middle. I pulled to one side, death pulled to the other. The flag moved back and forth. It lasted for some time but I had amazing strength and didn't want to let it go.

In one moment everything stopped. Then the bright light appeared in front of me and asked 'Marina, are you ready to die?' I said, 'No, no. I'm only 16 years old and I still haven't done anything good." Then I felt that I was going back to life. Death gave up on me.[8]

Later, in surgery, I left again. This time I was in a cold, cave-like tunnel with water running down the walls. I looked ahead down the tunnel and an awful heat hit my face, taking my breath away, choking me. I could see people reaching out of the bottom of the tunnel for me. I remember wanting to give them a drink of the water that was running down the walls but I was told I could not. Then I was told that I was not going to die now, but that I had been shown both sides of the afterlife and it was up to me to choose which place I would eventually go to. I realized I was being given another chance.[9]

With great speed, I was sucked downward into a dark void. The speed slowed and I became aware that this was because I was being resuscitation while going through a great mass of unfortunate, angry and mean souls. They wanted to keep me there. But each time my heart was resuscitated, with a hard shock I was back in my body. If they stopped resuscitation for even a few seconds, I was back in the dark void with the unfortunate souls. I kept thinking, 'Please don't stop resuscitating me.'

After waking up from this hellish experience during my coma, I turned my whole life around. This experience convinced me that the soul, after this life goes to a place I had earned by the things I had done during my life. I realized suddenly that this is my life and only I am responsible for how I handle things that come my way. I didn't always choose what comes my way, but I do choose how I deal with situations.[10]

Though I was also shown a much darker place where people did not seem to know that they had moved out of their bodies and continually fought each other for material things. Material possessions were their focus and all the actions were self-based there. Above them were also a legion of beings waiting. Whenever someone looked up and asked God for help they were whisked away to another place, a place more peaceful and tuned to God and God's love. But many seemed lost in this place, never looking up and never asking for help.[11]

I would love to say that my awareness then moved into a very serene, love-filled space, to be with the presence of an all-loving, forgiving entity. But that was not the case. Instead, my awareness moved from the physical world of the operating theater in Los Angeles and the kitchen conversation in India to a place where a great wild fire was raging. Dark entities with two horns and crooked teeth were running about.

I was taken to this place screaming and fighting. There was lightning in dark clouds. A perpetual, fierce storm raged. There was the smell of meat burning. It did not take long to realize that I was in Hell. It was excruciatingly painful. I could hear other souls screaming and suffering. Needles were being poked into me and I was being badly tortured. I was made to lie on a bed made of nails. Blood was oozing from various wounds.

I kept wondering what I had done in this life or past lives to deserve such punishment? As I experienced this horror, I began to have the strong awareness that my life had been very materialistic. Everything had been about me. When I met someone, I always asked myself "what can I get from this person?" The truth dawned on me in Hell that my life on Earth was devoid of love. I was not practicing compassion or forgiveness towards myself or others. I had a tendency to be especially harsh towards people that I perceived to be lower than me in social or professional status or hierarchies.

I remember feeling deeply sorry for the lack of kindness in my behavior and wishing I had done things differently. Immediately, as these realizations became crystal clear to me, this place — Hell — began to fade away.[12]

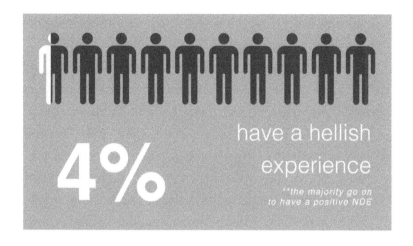

Crossover Retrospective Compilation[13]

OBSERVATIONS

DJK

• Hellish near-death experiences are rarely recorded. Both the prospective and retrospective studies show rates from 1% to 4% (see graphs in chapter 4). However, that is the reported rate. It is not likely those having a hellish experience would be as eager to report these at the same rate as those who have had a very positive experience. They may have also had success in burying the memory of their experience altogether. It should also be noted that a large percentage of those having reported a hellish NDE went on to have a positive one.

• The most common location for the occurrence of a hellish experience is in or around the tunnel, which may morph into a cave. It is most often described as dark or pitch-black. NDErs typically arrive there in an unsettling or frightening way — whether from their out-of-body experience or directly as they enter a state of clinical death.

• Those encountering this realm report seeing evil demons, slithering beings, and angry, mean souls. They report hands reaching out towards them in an attempt to pull them into a space that is often dark and obscured. They often report being attacked, badly injured, and even tortured. Screaming, moaning, and evil laughter is heard. They also report unpleasant odors such as a burning smell.

• Many describe calling out to a higher being for help, who often arrives in some form, causing these evil entities to flee. We do not get a sense of how long these encounters last, but they appear shorter than the average positive NDEs.

• The message NDErs often take away from a hellish experience is that they were shown this realm as a warning that they need to look more closely at how they have been living their lives, and how they have treated others. Unlike in the life-review, there does seem to be a sense of judgment. And the message from a hellish NDE is delivered more through fear than through a connection with others.

• Because the message is not delivered in a more direct way as in the life-review, the hellish experience leaves its message more up for interpretation. If it is not processed as an urgent message, but condemnation, it may have a more detrimental effect on the NDEr when they return, particularly if it is not processed with the help of another NDEr who came away with a deeper understanding of judgment, punishment, and the existence of hell.

<u>GS</u>

• Hellish NDEs are rare in the historical and cross-cultural NDE accounts, especially in indigenous societies. I think it's also worth mentioning that negative NDEs are not generally consistent with each other. There are no identifiable, negative, cross-cultural NDE features. This is in contrast to the general similarities of the more usual NDEs, even despite the cultural differences (entering darkness, emerging into light, meeting deceased relatives, etc.). To follow are a number of such NDEs where you will see extremely divergent experiences:

• The earliest recorded Native American NDE was a negative one. Reported in the 16th century, it involved a "wicked man" who had been "dead and buried," then revived. He claimed that his soul had journeyed westward toward the hellish realm of Popogusso, but was saved by a deity who made him return to his body in order to teach his people how to avoid such negative fates.

• An African account of the Akan people from the kingdom of Whydah (Benin) told of "an old Sorceress" who saw "strange things concerning Hell" after claiming "to have been there in person." She saw "several of her acquaintance[s] there," some being "miserably tormented." This was reported in 1704.

• Another African account comes from the Tswana (Botswana) people, reported in the 1920s. A lapsed Christian convert died and went to the spirit realm, where "she felt a flame of fire burning in her breast and causing her such distress as she had never experienced on earth." She saw a deceased aunt and cried out for water, but was given none. Then she saw Jesus "and the flame was quenched within her." He explained that the fire was an inevitable punishment for those who drink alcohol, for it drives away the Holy Spirit. On her return, the woman was shown a rock painted yellow, black, and white, though she was not told the meaning of it. She was, however, told, "that she would die before sunset; and she did." The missionary who reported the NDE suggested that much of the imagery was a result of pain caused by the woman's inflamed lungs, her own predilection for a drink, and from a sermon she had attended.

• In an account from 1646, a Native American woman of the Wyandot people had converted to Christianity before her NDE. When she rose from her burial in a Christian cemetery, she told of her experiences in the heaven of the French — a realm of fire where Christians burned souls in order to possess them. She was greeted "with fire-brands and burning torches, with cruelties and torments inconceivable." Though she was dead only one day, it seemed like years. She was finally assisted by "a certain person, moved with compassion for her," who released her from her chains and showed her a valley that led to the afterlife realm of indigenous people who had *not* converted to Christianity — a place of delight and goodness, a place without evil.

• In 1901, an elderly man of the A'aninin people reported a frightening and apparently hallucinatory NDE he had when young. While his body was being prepared for burial, he headed north to Cypress Hills where he was chased and caught by a small bear, which clung to his leg. At an enormous camp along a creek, naked men and women caught the boy in order to eat him. He escaped and returned to his body.

• In both medieval Chinese and medieval European NDEs, hellish experiences are sometimes described in great detail. But the contexts of them are overtly religious, essentially proselytizing, moralizing texts to encourage belief and positive behavior. As such, they need to be treated with caution. It's not clear when they might be fully invented, or when there may have been an actual NDE upon which they were based.

• An interesting, more recent example: in the mid-20th century, the French ballet dancer/director Janine Charrat reported a hellish NDE in a realm of flames, which she deliberately reduced to a soothing translucent rosiness when she became aware as in a lucid dream.

PvL

• Most frightening experiences occur before entering the tunnel, or before entering the otherworldly realm. About 15% of the people who have a positive NDE experience a frightening moment in the dark space before entering the tunnel and the light. It is as if they experience an incomplete NDE because they are not yet permitted to proceed into the light.

• One to two percent of people with a near-death experience linger in this frightening dark space, unable to escape. To their horror, they sometimes find themselves pulled even deeper into the profound darkness. The NDE ends in this scary atmosphere from where people reenter their body. The experience is devoid of positive emotions and later stirs profound feelings of guilt. In fact, such a terrifying NDE usually produces long-lasting emotional trauma. Not surprisingly, it is also known as a "hell experience." The exact number of people who experience such a frightening NDE is unknown because they often keep quiet, perhaps out of shame and guilt. However, if people can accept and make sense of this negative experience, they, too, eventually exhibit positive change.

EIGHTEEN

Religion on the Other Side

FINGERS POINTING TO THE MOON

This is my simple religion. There is no need for temples; no need for complicated philosophy. Our own brain, our own heart is our temple; the philosophy is kindness.

DALAI LAMA

I found myself in a city and was told that this was the City of God. I was at a water fountain with a man in a long white linen robe tied around the waist with a chord. He told me I could ask any question I wanted and said he would take me on a tour.

Because I had been raised at a time where Catholics said to even go into another Christian church was a mortal sin, and Lutherans said that those Catholics were going to go Hell because they had statuary in their churches and prayed to saints, I had a very pressing question. The first question I asked was, 'What is the right religion?' I was told, 'They all are. Each religion is a pathway trying to reach the same place.' I was shown a mountain, with each religious group trying to reach the top, separated from each other by distance, but each one was trying to get to the same place.

I was then told that people choose to be born into whichever religion or group that will help them achieve the lessons they are sent here to learn. I was told that the Earth is like a big school, a place where you can apply spiritual lessons learned and test yourself, under pressure, to see if you can actually 'live' what you already know you should do.

Basically, the Earth is a place to walk the walk and literally live the way it should be done. It was made clear to me that some people come to the Earth to work on only one aspect of themselves, while others come to work on several aspects. Then there are others who come to not only work on their own nature, but also to help the World as a whole.[1]

I saw things I never have seen before and have this feeling that we as followers of Christ have been fooled by the so-called men of God that preach in our churches. I really think its all about the money in most churches[2]

My hearing was more like I was joined with God's mind and I was part of God. I immediately knew things and He wanted to share things I needed to help me live and to help others. The space between heaven and earth is only in our minds. We are able to join God and His life here on earth; we are one.

I attend a non- denominational Christian church. However I can no longer believe that non-Christians are not accepted in heaven since I was told there was no condemnation and no judgement during my NDE. At the time I believed that people who didn't believe in Christ were condemned to hell. Since my NDE I believe there is no condemnation. We may choose to turn from God but God does not turn from us.

I believed that my life depended on me doing the right thing and trying to be a different person. I now believe life is about loving and sharing my God given gifts with myself and others. I was shown parts of my past and how God intervened and cared for me. I was told and shown that He is always caring for me. That worry is a waste of time. That there is no condemnation. That I am going to return someday and enjoy the utter joy and peace of heaven forever.[3]

I remember spontaneously appearing with no body in a formless place. Only beings of pure consciousness melding with one another were there, along with my consciousness. Those beings directly communicated with me through some kind of intuition, not through thought. I was Catholic at the time of my death, but I sure didn't see any god or Jesus... Now that I am Buddhist, My experiences match that of the Buddhist Heavens.[4]

I am still catholic because it is a little less fanatical but I have a different view regarding the beliefs of others. I believe God approaches you according to your individual beliefs, that we are all his children and He speaks to us according to the language that we understand. I do not believe in everlasting damnation for those with different beliefs. I think that hell exists only for those who voluntarily choose to distance themselves from God.[5]

For a few brief moments, I found myself in what seemed like 'heaven's front yard'. I was aware of a door to the right. Jesus (I am specific here) was talking to someone standing in front of me. I was amazed at the grace, unconditional love, and freedom I was feeling. This person had not been a Christian (by religion, or birth) on earth, but was given the opportunity to choose now. I thought this was fantastic.

I was in a short line, speaking to Jesus. Amazingly, he took as much time with each person as needed. I learned a lot from listening to the conversation of the person in front of me. It was clear I would be passing through a doorway or portal to 'heaven', but then the experience was over.[6]

Jesus said, 'I am the Light...' I used to think that was a metaphor, but my experience of heaven and God was of Light and energy.[7]

I believed in my Heart that God was a loving God and that His love would be expressed in miraculous ways. I believed that life continued after death. I didn't believe I was going to Hell like I was taught as a child in the Southern Baptist religion. I never had a good handle on what the after-life was going to be like, or what our spiritual bodies would look like, or how we would communicate.

This unfolded beautifully in my NDE. There is no judgement like the religions preach. The only time that I felt anything other than love, bliss, and joy was when I brought the question into the NDE. There was no judgement by God.[8]

I don't know what other people's experience would be. Mine was a Christian experience. There's no question. There are people, very few people — and those people are even less motivated to talk about it — who have experienced a hell or a darkness, an emptiness. That wasn't my experience, and so I don't know anything about it. God is way greater than anything we are able to conceive of.

I think human beings want to create a box and put God inside the box, because that way they can define God and control the outcome. But I've come to realize that God is way bigger than that. God truly loves every one of us, even the people that we don't love and don't think should be loved. God loves that person just as much as he loves us.

It's a very complex discussion, but many human

beings would like to think that justice means, "I'm in, and you're out, and you're out because you haven't done what I understand should be the thing that gets you into heaven. But God knows the heart of each one of us, and the God of the New Testament is not going to turn his back on a person who, for circumstances out of their control, has not developed that relationship in the here and now.

It is outrageous to think that a just and loving God is going to turn his back on the person who is so mentally handicapped that they don't even know what you're talking about when you talk about faith. Or the young altar boy who is so in love with God but gets abused, and he turns to a life of drugs and alcohol. It would be very easy to say, "That boy is out." Well, God understands that boy's heart and life.

For that matter, God understands the heart of the priest who abused him. I think it's time for us to get out of the business of judging. It's easy to be a Christian in America. It's really easy. But I think that most of us, if we grew up in a devoutly Muslim household in Afghanistan where 98 percent of the people are Muslim, would be Muslim. That's just the reality of it. And for us to pretend that God doesn't love those people because they happen to be in that situation is putting our own narrowness on a God who is bigger than we are.

That is not to say that everything is good and everything is accepted and we're all in. But I'm not going to pretend I know the answers to all the questions. And I think it's disingenuous for us to claim the God of the New Testament and the covenant of love and forgiveness, and at the same time turn our own backs on people who haven't had the opportunity to understand what that means.[9]

I was raised Jewish and what we were taught about the afterlife was definitely not what I experienced or I learned. I learned that we are here many times. An afterlife definitely exists. I now know how this game on earth goes, why we're here, what we need to do and that if we don't learn the lessons we need to learn, we have to go and do it once more until we have the complete, earthly experience mastered.

We have many lives and many experiences. It's all about picking what lesson you want to learn, learning them, and moving on to a higher source of consciousness. I learned we are all one giant collective of conscious humans. It's like a school. We are all here learning and having these human experiences.[10]

All of the sudden I was surrounded by pure, bright, brilliant, Heaven white. It was white, but not earthly white. Seriously, there are no words that can explain the beauty of colors in Heaven. I was in a cell. It was made of brown metal. I had a tan 'potato bag' on my body as a form of clothing. I had brown leather bands 'belts' around my neck, waist, wrists and ankles. I believe at first I was somewhat confused. There was love all around me. Much more love than a person can feel here on earth. One by one, those thick brown bands fell off. The door to the 'cell' opened. I walked out and fell to my knees. I couldn't look up. I knew it was Jesus. I was in the presence of the Lord. It was at that time that we were telepathically communicating. I was asking and crying about things that happened to me from the beginning of my life for the most part. (Incest, emotional abuse, physical abuse, mental abuse, running away starting at about twelve years old to get away from all the abuse. Stranger raped at fourteen. Countless things happened to me, but this might give the reader an idea as to where I came from. Frankly, I believe I was living a hell on earth.) It was amazing and beautiful. My Savior answered, giving me knowledge and peace about every single thing that had happened to me. Everything. However, He didn't allow me to come back with all of that He revealed to me. What He did, is sent me back with peace in my spirit. Bondages gone. I am a brand new person on the inside. I have been set completely free of my past. I truly believe that He knew I was on a one way ticket to hell, and because of me crying out to Him he answered my prayers!! That is how much He loves me.[11]

I now know beyond a shadow of a doubt that my life will not end with my 'death' and that a great presence exists; though I do not attempt to fit it with my previous religious beliefs as I think that religions here only have a scant few details of what really lies beyond this mortal existence.

When I see and hear people speak in the name of religion, after experiencing what lies beyond, it is evident to me that in all instances thus far, people are merely reciting what they have been taught and told to believe. Very little seems to mesh with my experience outside of the feeling that life beyond will be sublimely peaceful and full of love and that a great person or being of some sort is responsible for and created what we will experience on 'the other side'.

I possess a deep belief in the events and feelings that I experienced and know that that beauty only awaits me as a reward for living a life of kindness, humility and compassion towards others. In that regard I feel a very strong connection to all life, be it plants, animals and specifically humans.[12]

At some distance, I could see some people standing in a circle, this time I could see all of them. It was around 8 to 10 people. Then I saw a huge light in the center of the hall and I started drifting towards it. There was a huge light coming in from that huge hole. I am a fervent Hindu with blind faith in the Super Power.

To be more specific, I firmly believe in our Goddess, Mother Kaalika. I could feel that she was there on the other side of that beam of bright light coming from outside the hall. I was happy to know that she was there outside. I bowed and tried to see her. As a Hindu Brahmin, we are taught that Heaven and hell both exist - what on the other hand I saw was happy faces only.

The inconsistency was not seeing any heaven or hell. I could feel (is it a right word, don't know) that my Goddess Kalika is there on the other side of that beam of bright light that was coming from outside the hall. I was happy to know that she is there outside.[13]

The light was literally blinding, but I could stare directly into it without flinching. I felt as though - I all of a sudden knew everything there was to know about everything and I felt this enormous presence of love and respect and everything good.

Artistic portrayals of Jesus began flashing before my eyes, all different kinds of pictures and paintings and I saw a sequence of the crucifixion of Christ. The light was getting brighter at this time, and wider. Soon Jesus appeared in front of me and I could do nothing but fall to my knees and then lay my head on the floor at his feet.

It was like that for an eternity and then Jesus said, 'You are worthy child, rise.' So I did and faced the Lord Jesus Christ with utmost guilt and feelings of utter insignificance. Jesus said, 'You have learned from your mistakes, my child. You will return, and you will show others the way. You will spread the love of God.' I immediately began to weep uncontrollably (yes even though I'm a seventeen year old dude) and kept saying, 'I am unworthy Lord.'

At this moment, I was in the presence of my deceased relatives, two uncles, an aunt, a grandfather and a great-grandmother of whom none spoke but they pointed to the 'ground', indicating I must return. At this point, I was spontaneously in my mortal body in the hospital looking up at my parents and friends. They would never believe the story.[14]

All of us are still learning and it is okay. It is okay to make mistakes and we do not need to, nor should we, judge each other. Each one is doing what they must do to continue the learning and testing they were put here to do. My Christian-molded background might have led to certain expectations but none of my experience was near to what is taught.

I could see how different religions might try to explain all that I saw and felt, but there was so much more than any of them promote. My experience was something of a conglomerate of many religions though not following any specific doctrinal ideal or image. It is like all of them might have a piece of the whole, but not all.

What became crystalline clear to me during these experiences is that the problem comes more in how man interprets religion than in the religion itself. What I saw was so much more than one religion. However, there also seemed to be purpose in all of the religions and people are drawn to the ones that would help them most with whatever 'theme' their life purpose happens to be in this lifetime.[15]

I have written about it in different ways many times. I have talked with people about it over the years. It is a vast subject for me. And it is very simple, as well. The Buddha, The Christ and others have all summed it up in very simple terms. Be here now. Love is all there is. Life is a dream. The vastness - the source is beyond our comprehension.[16]

OBSERVATIONS

DJ

• When given the opportunity to ask a question of God or Jesus in a near-death experience, the two most common are: why do we exist, and which is the one "true" religion? To the first question, it is explained that we exist simply to love one another. And to the second — there are different paths to God, but at their core, they are all the same. Two important questions, one clear and simple answer. It always comes back to love.

• In terms of a belief in God, NDErs experiencing this realm run the gamut from the religious, to the spiritual, to the atheist, to the agnostic. If there is movement away from a current belief system, it would hue towards a more general, inclusive spirituality. Those who more strongly associate with a particular religion or spiritual discipline may hold on to their general tenants, but with less of an attachment to their more institutional elements. Others still will become deeper in their existing faith.

• Almost universally, NDErs no longer accept that only those that come from a particular religion or spiritual tradition can reach heaven. They have experienced firsthand that God does not judge, and that all are welcome in this realm.

<u>GS</u>

• There are NDE experiencer groups on Facebook and people who attend the International Association of Near-Death Studies (IANDS) conferences who are adamant that NDE experiences of Jesus, like their own, are the only true, "real" ones. Some even say the rest are deceptions arranged by Satan. This view does not align with the massive database of retrospective studies or the prospective studies that target this question.

• Some of the Native American examples, among others, show indigenous people challenging the teachings of missionaries. They believed the eye-witness accounts of their own people who had been to the otherworld and returned over the teachings of the foreign missionaries. They even were able to argue with them on points of logic.

• While NDEs are universal, and people commonly base certain religious beliefs on them, they do so only when their cultural environment allows, unless they are innovating away from established tradition. Local attitudes toward death affect receptivity to NDE phenomena.

• In addition to providing a well of symbols with which to express and interpret NDEs, a culture and its environment also impose limitations on such expressions.

• Indigenous statements about beliefs often refer to an experience not only as the source and authority of the belief, but also as the actual descriptor of it. In some cases, the only statement of belief on record is an account of an NDE, implicitly supporting the experiential source hypothesis.

• The numerous examples of NDEs that run contrary

to local or personal beliefs demonstrate not only that these experiences are not predicated on cultural expectation, but also that they often lead to a spiritual or religious reorientation. Experiential validation is important to the establishment of new beliefs and the maintenance of existing ones and is thus itself a factor in the formation of religions.

• Whatever the ultimate nature of the prompting event — neurophysiological, metaphysical, or something else — NDEs are powerful generators of religious beliefs in an afterlife, both for individuals and in established religious traditions. While not every religious system shares similar afterlife conceptions, and though some have none at all, cross-cultural, structural similarities are so widespread that it is tempting to speculate an NDE element for the afterlife journey conceptions, even in the absence of a documentary example.

• Near-death experiences provide one way for unaffiliated spiritual (not religious people) to find a community with certain common beliefs. Normally the preserve of organized religions.

• There are NDEs of atheists and very young children who have either no prior beliefs or totally opposite beliefs to what they actually experience. But we still have all this information and knowledge floating around in our heads. I'm not saying we're creating the experience, but I am saying we act as filters for it. I don't think we can get rid of all of the cultural clutter. Maybe there are moments during the experience that are like a pure consciousness event where there's no content going on in the mind. Overall, however, when we come back and try to explain what the experience was like, we don't have any language other than the cultural language that we have. So we are going to use metaphors. We are going to use symbols, ones drawn from our culture and language.

PvL

• A near-death experience can sometimes engender profound religious feelings and give people the impression of a personal bond with God. An NDE can lead some people to believe that they are one of God's chosen. This sense of salvation can make them feel relatively invulnerable and extremely important and may result in a strong urge to spread the word of the NDE as a deeply religious experience. Such proselytizing is often seen as intrusive and stirs a great deal of resistance. But generally speaking, people's religious sentiment increases after an NDE while their interest in organized religion declines sharply.[17]

• A near-death experience can evoke the sense that the old self has died and that a new person has been born. The NDE and its subsequent changes are thus experienced as a spiritual death and rebirth.[18]

• If religious affiliation declines, people also report an increase in religiosity and a greater interest in spirituality, meditation, prayer, and surrender.

• With their precious life restored, people view themselves as having a unique mission and are fueled by a heightened sense of spiritual purpose. They feel part of a meaningful universe and adopt a more philosophical attitude to life.

NINETEEN

How NDEs Change Everyone

.

Death is simply a shedding of the physical body like the butterfly shedding its cocoon. It is a transition to a higher state of consciousness where you continue to perceive, to understand, to laugh, and to be able to grow.

ELIZABETH KUBLER-ROSS

I learned that the only thing in life is unconditional love. I also sensed or knew that a son who I lost in an accident at the age of thirty-two was safe and in the light. I know now that death is not the end - there is life after death.

I have a minor in Bible from Abilene Christian University; I'm lost now and am having trouble understanding some of the teachings of my religion. People around me say my personality has changed, I am more compassionate and understanding, things that used to be important don't mean anything anymore.

I am more emotional, have a deeper sense of feelings for others; I care more for the plights of others.... I now believe that everyone returns to the light which is God. I also believe that all have been here before in a past life or lives. This goes against all my previous beliefs, having a real problem in this area. But who am I to question the love and the power of God? All things are possible.[1]

———

I was sent back from five NDE experiences for a reason and that is to live out the rest of my life only to serve Him. Because of my experience with NDE, I retired this year to give my life to others by writing a book to enlighten others that as the movie declared 'God Is Not Dead.' As a neuro-scientist with brain anoxia, specializing in brain trauma I plan to devote the rest of my life in helping our veterans with post-traumatic head injuries.[2]

———

The whole thing was meaningful and significant. It changed my life forever for the good. My wife would always say she knew I loved her. But she always felt I never really 'needed' her. She said that now I make her feel important, make her feel loved, make her feel needed, and that my life would be meaningless without her in it. And I do.

I was always cocky, arrogant, self-centered and aggres-sive. Now, I am calm, patient, understanding, loving, empathetic, sympathetic, and compassionate and have a zest for life, and the people in it. I used to be a contractor chasing after the almighty dollar. After the accident, I closed my company and started work in the social service field. I work with disadvantaged children and families helping them to overcome the hurdles, which stand in their way in order to make their lives more complete and happy.

I now make in two weeks what it would take me a day and a half to earn before. I'm able to make my life experiences, knowledge and skills work for other people. I'm good at what I do, and that's what God wanted me to come back and do. I'm doing it. And it's hard work, but it's very rewarding.[3]

I lost connection with all of my friends. I was unable to do the social interactions that I used to do. Communication dropped off completely. I was in my own little world trying to put the pieces of the puzzle together. I resigned from my 22 year career in Financial Technology. I dropped all communication with my co-workers. I would read books all day long. I learned about Crystals and how to create Orgone Pyramids. Today, I am an Artist. My relationship with my wife is on thin ice. That part has been sad. I hope it works out. She says I am a totally different person. She's right. I am.[4]

There is another world, place, and people I loved are waiting for me. I think my life has been harder since because I feel I am out of step with the world.... My anger has changed. I feel still as if I should not be here - like my time here is limited and I have no problem with passing over. I have no fear of death at all - almost like death is the beginning. [5]

In the days after the event, normal physical life felt convoluted and imaginary, almost surreal. Normal life seemed much more like a perpetual dream-state than the time spent outside of my body. It was if I had slipped back into a dream when I returned to my body and I still recall the event so vividly that even today events in my daily life feel discombobulated, random and without purpose. / When I think about the event I can still recall the same feeling of intense lucidity. If I close my eyes and focus on the mental imagery, it feels as if it only happened a few short weeks ago. I am able to recall every detail of the event except for the feelings of love, peace and warmth I felt as I was enveloped by the intense light. [6]

During the first year, I tried to forget what I had seen. Sometimes I tried to drink it away, but that just seemed to make it more vivid. I stopped drinking or taking anything stronger than aspirin and then started to feel at peace with the memory of it.

I started to feel like I had been given a gift of great value, spiritually. My husband thought I was crazy, so I divorced him. Now, I'm happy with who I am, all by myself. I can no longer feel individual love. Like man and wife kind of love. I feel the same love for everybody. I treat them all the same. I do not date or have any intimate relationships.[7]

I will say that I have a forgiving feeling of myself and my decisions. I have a forgiving feeling towards anyone in my life that I had previously held contempt for. I do not anger easily now, like in the past. I understand life lessons I have had, and why others treated me the way they did. I understand my decisions I made and how it was needed to affect others - we are in this together. Your enemy is your friend. I have more patience and understanding. I don't view the 'bad' things as bad, and the 'good' things as good. They just are because they need to be.

I have had marital issues, because I have changed and find importance in other things than my spouse. It isn't bad; it is just different. It is no one's fault we are not connecting on a spiritual level, which has now become of great importance to me. He has given me space to be me, which is helping tremendously.[8]

I just knew that this reality was, because of the knowledge and understanding about things I had questions about and things I never even thought of. I now know I was over, it happened, I knew, I had knowledge I never had before. I only regret losing a lot of it only remembering bits and pieces. [9]

An afterlife definitely exists. I am and was raised as a Catholic. But, I know that we have many, many lives. Where I am confused is if I actually experience these lives or if I am tuned into these lives (much like someone tuning a radio to a frequency). The experience is real, more real than one can simple imagine. There's just way too much detail to be conjured up. I have learned to keep my experience to myself because most people have difficulty accepting it. [10]

My past flashed before me, out of my control. I will not discuss in detail my life review. But, I will say that I have a forgiving feeling of myself and my decisions. I have a forgiving feeling towards anyone in my life that I had previously held contempt for. I do not anger easily now, like in the past. I understand life lessons I have had, and why others treated me the way they did. I understand my decisions I made and how it was needed to affect others - we are in this together. Your enemy is your friend.

I have more patience and understanding. I don't view the 'bad' things as bad, and the 'good' things as good. They just are because they need to be. I have had marital issues, because I have changed and find importance in other things than my spouse. It isn't bad; it is just different. It is no one's fault we are not connecting on a spiritual level, which has now become of great importance to me. He has given me space to be me, which is helping tremendously.[11]

My past flashed before me, out of my control. There is another world, place, and people I loved are waiting for me. I think my life has been harder since because I feel I am out of step with the world.... My anger has changed. I feel still as if I should not be here - like my time here is limited and I have no problem with passing over. I have no fear of death at all - almost like death is the beginning. [12]

Experience was definitely real I just knew that this reality was, because of the knowledge and understanding about things I had questions about and things I never even thought of. I now know I was over, it happened, I knew, I had knowledge I never had before. I only regret losing a lot of it only remembering bits and pieces.[13]

I woke up four days later as they were taking me to my room from the intensive care unit. Here's the problem. Nobody asked me how I felt about it. I loved it, of course, but I have so many questions. I cry at the drop of a hat. Everyone said that it was a wonderful experience and yes, it was, but it screwed me up in a way. I've kept my feelings about the whole ordeal bottled up for three years. I tell everyone about the experience. Joyously. I love my Jesus, but dang, what a ride. I feel and see things I can't explain. Sometimes I feel I'm going nuts.[14]

This experience changed my life. I woke up in awe, and it changed my outlook on life. When I woke up, I wanted to go right back there! No, I did not become suicidal, but I felt I could not wait to go back to that place. I have always been terrified about death. Now I am excited about it.[15]

I thought heaven would be different. I'd always imagined a magical kingdom of a more earthly nature. I had thought my grandmother or someone else I knew who had gone before me or that Jesus would come to me and take me with Him and he'd greet me. I believed I'd see Jesus and it did not occur to me that perhaps God is one and is simply known by many names.

I thought I'd remain as my 'heavenly body' and me would still look like 'the me' I knew. It was very different from what I had always thought and was taught it would be. I thought there would be trillions of angels singing in a choir. There was music, but not like what we know as music. It was just part of everything. Life can be brutal at times and sometimes it's hard to remember such joy and not be present in it. Other times remembering is a comfort and gives me hope. There are also times when I come close to feeling here and now what it felt like to be in heaven. There are times that I remember that heaven and God are right here within us and all around us.

Over all, I never doubt that I am loved. I don't know everything, now that I am here again. But my memories of my time in heaven are more vivid to me that anything else I have experienced before or since then. It was the defining experience of my life. Prior to dying, I felt very awkward and uncomfortable with someone who was experiencing grief or any type of crisis. That changed for me, I changed.[16]

I know I went into the light. The feelings, emotions and love experienced were real. I still find it hard to understand why I'm still here. It's like I'm caught between two worlds.[17]

I believe the most important change is to see life in a different way. Fashions, money, social life, appearances, are now no longer important. What is important is the means to live comfortably, but not to live solely to obtain them. I realized that the things I need, I will receive as a consequence of living a good life. To see and love others in spite of whom they are or what they do, is something that isn't as difficult as before.

I have become compassionate, understanding and, in my mind, I always try to deal with those that are harmful by trying to make them see that it is not necessary to fight or to inflict damage. I have VERY many conversations with myself all the time. Always trying to understand what is happening to someone else, and put myself in their place. It's very complex.[18]

In that state I discovered that the only important thing is LOVE. From that moment on, I love people much more intensely (since the experience I created a charitable institution which is now a foundation). I also love myself very much, something I had completely forgotten to do during my intensive professional life because the only luggage we can take with us from this life is what we do out of love for others and ourselves. Our soul is made for LOVE, and from that realization, I understand we are happy here when we love and unhappy when we practice 'unlove' (hate, rancor, envy, etc.)[19]

The experience has left me with this feeling of being in limbo. Like, 'Why me?' I realize that we are without age. We have existed from the beginning, and we are without end. We are immortal. Nothing dies, it just transforms. We are perfection in the eye of the Creator.[20]

I find most of my old friends pedantic and annoying - I have become more isolated. I prefer to be alone or with my children - except I have this huge need to make a difference and help people in a real way. I volunteer at the homeless shelter and am pursuing an emergency medical technician certification - even though it pays one fifth of my current salary, I have become rather illogical as far as seeking material gain. I can't seem to purchase anything that I enjoy and prefer to just give it away.[21]

I no longer fear death. I wish I could say I live without worry but even though I know it's unnecessary I still have it. I have a connection with God and others that is very personal and is forever. It's not limited to this earth. I don't see life or death the same. I miss people who die but I am thrilled that they are at peace and no longer suffering the limits of this life.[22]

Not to lie, but to stand by myself and take care of myself. I learned to be true to my own values and myself, to forgive without accepting negative actions from others, to let go and forgive, and to stay in joy. I also learned to be in the present as much as possible, to nourish myself and to be my own best friend, and to be a good friend to others.

We all have our own path to learn and work on accepting this so I try not brooding over problems, but to let go of them even when it's difficult. I try to address the challenges and problems again when I have the strength to overcome them, to forgive myself and not push myself too much, to feel myself more and not cross my own limits and values, to be good and honor ALL living. I learned that death, that to die is so amazingly beautiful and full of joy and love.[23]

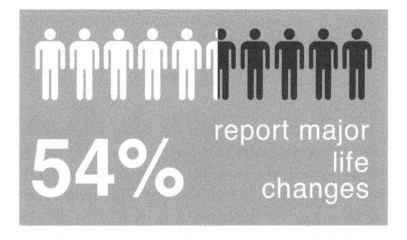

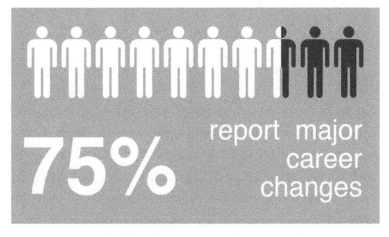

CROSSOVER [24] - *CROSSOVER* [25]

OBSERVATIONS

DJK

For more than 50 years, we have come to better understand the dramatic impact a near-death experience has on an individual. The thousands of written and oral testimonials have made that abundantly clear. What has not been fully studied is the impact the NDE has on those who have not had a near-death experience, but invested the time in trying to understand the phenomenon. Through attending lectures, listening to interviews and testimonials, watching documentary films, and reading books such as the one in your hands. And perhaps meeting and speaking directly with someone who has had a near-death experience themselves.

I suspect the majority who have made this effort have been changed in some way, likely for the better. I would count myself among this group, which is no small feat for a self-proclaimed skeptic and quantum economist.

I have come to have a different, and I would say healthier and more informed, understanding of death, the process of dying, and the possibility of an afterlife. I feel I have a better sense of why I have been tested the way I have throughout my life. The purpose behind great joy and sadness I have experienced. The value of my defeats as well as my successes. And of course, I have discovered the focus of why I am here — at its core — which is simply to love and to learn. We are all one. That is the insight and message repeated over, and over, and over.

The consistency in message and experience that is

brought back with an NDEr has been paramount in my conviction. No less important is the dramatic impact it has on the NDEr — in real-time and over the course of a life. It is the near-death experiencer's absolute certainty that what they experienced was "more real than real" that has left a lasting impression on me. I see it in the expression on their face, hear it in the inflection in their voice, and am continually amazed by the consistency of experience across race, gender, religious belief, and culture.

They say God does not play dice. They say there is a reason for everything. There are no coincidences. I believe that in principle. So why are reports of NDEs coming in such high numbers these last several decades? Why has this subject so clearly pierced our collective consciousness now? Yes, resuscitation techniques first employed in the 1960s have made it possible to bring those who are clinically dead back to life — something that was not possible before this time. And yes, our growing understanding of quantum physics gives us insight into how something like an NDE can theoretically occur. But that does not answer the question — why now? This is the question that lingers for me.

The nature of the near-death experience tells us the major themes that occur during an NDE will not change. The space that appears to offer the greatest opportunity to deepen our understanding of the NDE, barring a major advancement in quantum mechanics, is in studying the fine details within the testimonials themselves. Sifting through each word and looking for those subtle nuances, just as those wise old blind men laying their hands on the elephant, will yield greater insight. No doubt you likely picked up on some small details in this book that you hadn't noticed before. Details that may alter or deepen your understanding of the NDE, as they certainly have for me.

As far as I am concerned, there is no subject or phenomenon that measures in importance to the near-death experience. How could there be? The NDE contains answers to life's most important questions —questions that mankind has struggled to understand throughout history. Like many of you, the near-death experience has changed me and my outlook on life and beyond. I feel very fortunate for that.

GS

I've approached my NDE research as a scholar rather than as a seeker on a personal spiritual quest. To me, a scholar is not a person of faith, but one of reason, logic, evidence, as well as a bit of imagination and creativity. This is also reflected in my personal life, because as a confirmed agnostic, I choose neither to believe nor to disbelieve in things I don't actually know. I'm content living in that "cloud of unknowing" when it comes to NDEs and other so-called supernatural phenomena. Like everyone else, the truth will be revealed to me soon enough!

Throughout my two decades of researching and writing about cross-cultural and historical near-death experiences, I've tried to remain on the sidelines of the debate as to whether or not they're genuine evidence of an afterlife. But of course, I would love to know the answer. I remember the feeling I had when I first read about NDEs: a horizon-expanding sense of awe and wonder, perhaps made even more profound because I had no religious faith. Anecdotal or otherwise, there seemed to be some evidence of an after-life from people who went there while temporarily dead or near death. If those experiences were real, what could be a more profound discovery about human existence?

For me, NDEs remain a mystery. It is the case, however, that none of the theories attempting to debunk NDEs, to explain them away in materialist terms, are at all convincing. In fact, the main problems with such theories are very much related to the subject of my research: none of them really addresses NDEs in all their similarities and all their differences across cultures.

Most reductionist theories of NDEs rely on some physiological cause resulting in a compromised brain-state. It has variously been argued that NDEs are caused by anoxia (lack of oxygen to the brain), hypoxia (too much oxygen in the brain), hypercarbia (too much carbon dioxide in the brain), temporal lobe epilepsy, anesthetics, REM intrusion, and so on. If this were the case, if NDEs were caused by physiological processes that invariably result in the same experiences, we would not expect to see such variation between accounts. Since the earliest days of near-death studies, researchers have been trying to pinpoint a set of core elements shared by all NDErs – and after almost 50 years, they have been unable to do so.

Not only do the differences between NDE accounts challenge the physiological theories, to my way of thinking, they might actually make it more likely that they're genuine afterlife experiences. After all, given the diversity of human experience on Earth – with all our cultural and individual uniqueness – why should we expect to suddenly all have exactly the same experience at death? I expand on this idea in my new book, The Next World: Extraordinary Experiences of the Afterlife (White Crow, 2022), where I explore the possibility that there are multiple kinds of afterlives for different people. In short, there is no reason to believe that our diversity would disappear simply because we are no longer housed in physical bodies.

By the same token, the mere cross-cultural existence of NDEs could also support the idea that they're genuine. This is especially the case when we consider that people in virtually all societies give them the same basic meaning: this is what happens when we die. It's also important that, despite all the diversity of accounts and the obvious cultural idiosyncrasies, NDEs everywhere draw upon the same general repertoire of sub-experiences. Just like a visit to a new city or exploring a large museum, our experiences will be both similar and different from each other depending on our interests, perceptions, background, beliefs, focus, etc.

While many would argue that there is no absolute, water-tight proof that NDEs are genuine afterlife experiences, there are a number of compelling cases that point in that direction. There are children who met deceased relatives they never knew they had, encounters with a person not known to have died whose recent death was later validated, congenitally blind people seeing for the first time during the experience, temporarily brain-dead patients accurately describing surgical procedures they witnessed while out of their bodies, and the seemingly miraculous positive transformations individuals so often exhibit following NDEs.

Reports like these give me the same sense of wonder and awe as that adolescent first reading about NDEs. While they may not convince me to the point of knowledge that NDEs are evidence of an afterlife, I would argue that they provide a perfectly reasonable, rational basis for such beliefs. After all, we as human beings base our knowledge on experiences. It's not surprising that we'd base our after-life beliefs on the most relevant kind of experience.

The study of NDEs has expanded my intellectual, spiritual, cultural, and creative horizons, opening my irreligious mind to possibility – to at least understanding what exactly I am "unknowing." Somehow along the way, just like those who've had an NDE, it has also made me wholly unafraid of death. Like many people, I fear the pain and suffering that the dying often go through. It feels tragic to contemplate leaving behind my loved ones, special places, personal things, travel, work, and all the rich experiences of life in a body on Earth. But I have no fear concerning the kinds of mental experiences I might have during or after my death. After all, even if the NDE is an illusion – a temporary state of wonder and bliss followed by oblivion – it suggests that death will be a gloriously transcendent adventure.

PvL

Like Dag Hammerskjöld writes, "Our ideas about death define how we live our life." As long as we believe that death is the end of everything we are, we will give our energy toward the temporary and material aspects of our

life. In our short-sightedness, and sometimes wilful igno-
rance, we forget to reflect on the future of our planet, and
where our children and our grandchildren will have to live
and survive. We forget about sustainability as we are now
systematically destroying and exhausting our planet. We
should realize that the harm we cause to each other and to
nature ultimately is harming ourselves, because we as
humans are not only intensively interconnected ('entan-
gled') with each other, but also with animals and plants
living on our endangered earth.

I hope that in the near future we will accept non-local
concepts to understand how we are, and always will be,
interconnected with each other, also after physical death,
and that we have to change our personal consciousness, not
only to change the way we live but also to change the way
we want to respect people who are willing and able to share
their NDE, ELE, or ADC with us. Their lives changed in
ways they were not prepared for, and they all tell us that
they fundamentally changed their ideas about life and
death, because, 'You can be physically dead but your mind
lives on.' Another quote: 'Death was not death, but another
form of life'.

Consciousness seems to be our essence, and once we
leave our body, leave our physical world, we exist as pure
consciousness, beyond time and space, and are we enfolded
in pure, unconditional love. Obviously, this new insight
helps us to better understand the idea of human consciousness beyond the brain. It will require a huge change in
consciousness indeed. We should all feel the responsibility
for this change.[26]

A FINAL THOUGHT

Now that you've trained your mind's eye to see those nuances — those nuggets of gold — what better way to utilize them than by journeying through another Crossover Experience in full — in all of its otherworldly glory? Don't rush through it. Slow down and experience each and every magical moment. Let yourself be there.

And remember that, one day, you will experience this journey, too.

TWENTY

A CROSSOVER EXPERIENCE II

"I WILL ONE DAY RETURN"

Finally I am dying. And breathing deeply for the first time, I see traces of God in everything.

DJ KADAGIAN

I realized I was floating above a car wreck. I had an altered type of vision because even though I was above the car I could 'see' inside the car with a sort of 'super vision'. I saw my body and I saw the body of my friend at the wheel. I had no real emotion to what I was witnessing.

There was a calm sense of detachment and I remember looking at my body as if it were a sweater or a suit I had worn and now had cast off. I remember thinking, 'That was cool being Thomas,' like it was some fun excursion, this human life.[1]

The craziest part for me was the feeling of overwhelming euphoria. I didn't feel foggy or messed up in the head. I felt extremely clear, conscious, and happy. I felt so happy that it freaks me out to remember it. It was like someone had just given me the best drug never invented. I didn't think about my parents or my life. There was no fear or any negative emotion at al. I feel SO good. I thought, 'THIS FEELS SO GOOD. I AM SO HAPPY!'

I looked around at the scene before me feeling surrounded by love and warmth. After a moment, I have no idea how long, my hearing returned. I could hear my friend Jessica's voice and other voices shouting. Only then did it occur to me that 'Oh yeah, I have a body in that other place right now. Man, I really like it here though. I don't know if I want to go back. This feels so good here.'

I tried to speak but it was more of a mental thought where I was trying to tell her, 'It's ok guys, stop freaking out. I'm fine here! Y'all are overreacting, this is great! I think I want to stay here for awhile longer actually and check this place out.' I was feeling so peaceful and wished I could communicate to them that I was fine. But I wasn't fine, I was dying. But that never occurred to me, because all I could think was that I was so happy there, that I didn't ever want to leave.[2]

It is hard for me to explain but I entered another plane of existence at the exact moment I passed out and realized I was floating in a multidimensional space. This was not a dream, dreams for me have never had well defined time and space relation or even make cognitive sense. I was one hundred percent aware of my mind in the situation. I was not quite sure or even asking at this point, where was I or why am I here? I was there, wherever there is.[3]

Then thoughts about my life entered my vision. I saw my mom's face and I thought that she'll be really sad if I stay here. She won't understand how amazing this place is. I never actually thought of it as 'this is life after death.' It was just, my body is over there somewhere, and I am here.[4]

I suddenly became aware that my heart and lungs were silent and thought to myself 'Now I really must have died, at least I am not in pain.' My soul or spirit left my body and I found myself floating in a dark space. I was not afraid. I felt comfortable there. I thought it was very beautiful.

I was still thinking like myself, feeling like myself. My memory and personality remained, and I could float in this space freely. I had something similar to my body but it was made of a transparent and milky substance. Like ghosts are described, with a slight glow. When I got bored of being there by myself without doing anything, I thought that there must be more than this. I asked God to take me where He was.[5]

Then I remember being transported up quickly and with light and swiftness that defied all things and I could no longer see the car accident. I couldn't see anything but it did not matter. Sight suddenly seemed like some primitive tool as I felt enveloped in some kind of 'knowing' that surpassed the human senses.[6]

I was able to breathe deeply and oxygenate myself. I didn't feel ill. I didn't hurt in any way, absolutely. I remember my parents and my husband. I knew that they were suffering, but I also knew they would be OK. I wanted to console them, love them more and more. Nothing, absolutely nothing worried me. It was as if I knew that sooner or later they would enjoy this excellent feeling of well-being that I had, and I stopped worrying.[7]

I found myself walking in a tunnel toward, well, I wasn't sure where, actually. I just know that this was a place of perfect peace, and totally without pain or sorrow. The tunnel wasn't really very long, perhaps one hundred and fifty to two hundred feet. It was pink, kind of rose-colored quartz crystal, and had stalactite and stalagmite formations along the walls.

At the end of the tunnel was a bright, pure light, purer than any I have ever seen anywhere. It was tall and narrow, and rounded at both ends...I had every sense of self, I was still me, and had the sense of walking in a body as I went up the tunnel. I had no fear, and no thought of what was happening to me. It seemed the thing to do was to walk up the tunnel.[8]

I felt drawn to the light and could not look away. As I stared at the point of light it gradually grew brighter and brighter. It filled the entire room with light so bright it filled every corner and nook until the room just faded away. I felt as if I was rushing towards a giant, intensely bright, round sphere and was overcome with a feeling of deep happiness and contentment.

It felt warm, though not in a temperature sort of way that I was accustomed to feeling with my skin, but rather warmth that permeated me to the core of my perceived 'self'. It was unlike anything I have ever felt before or since, but it was definitely a feeling of love. Not love in the sexual or intimate sense, but a love filled with understanding, acceptance and happiness.

Once encompassed by the brilliant white light, I was fully aware that I was no longer on Earth. Everything was so brilliantly white and bright that it felt as if I was blinded. I only know that it was a place that could not exist on Earth.

I had a deep sense of familiarity with what lay beyond the white light. It felt as though I was truly home after a long journey and that feeling imbued me with a sense of purpose, logic and order to the events that transpired in my life on Earth as well as all other people that came and went before me and those that would come after me.[9]

When I came through the light, I knew everyone there and they were so happy to see me: welcoming me home. They were all dead relatives I had never met before, but I knew everyone. They also appeared in human-form, to be recognized, but somehow I sensed that was not their true form now. I had a connection with everyone and almost a collective consciousness.[10]

My family from the beginning They were all around me. A thousand questions from as many voices, yet there was no confusion, just me telling them what I knew of the living. It wasn't like I was answering each question, either. It was more like my entire knowledge, my entire life and life experience had been poured out on a great table for all to see and pick through, and some specifics were addressed.[11]

I saw my grandmother, running with children, towards me. She took me by the hand and we were at the beginning of a bridge over a small creek. We talked for what seemed like hours about my life since she had died. I had just turned 9 years old when she died. We also talked about when she came to let me know that she died, to say goodbye until we would meet again and not to be sad. She was so vibrant and healthy, despite dying of a brain tumor. I told her how much I missed her and she said that she watches over my son and me....[12]

As I stood there in the garden, I noticed once again, how beautiful and brilliant the colors of the flowers, the trees and the grass were. The reds were redder, the pinks more pink, and yellows more yellow. The colors were so much more vibrant than any colors I had ever seen.

The air was sweetly fragrant. It was so clean and clear. The grass felt cool to the touch, like on a beautiful spring day. There were birds singing in the trees, and I saw a stream where the water glistened like diamonds in the sun as it flowed over the rocks. I heard music, which was more beautiful than anything I had ever heard before.

It was then that I noticed everything had its own pitch or sound. The trees had a sound, the leaves on the trees had their own sound, the grass had a sound, the rocks had their own sound, the water had yet another sound, and so on; and, when you take all of those individual sounds and put them all together, it sounded like the most magnificent symphony and choir ever created, and what's even more amazing, was, everything and everyone in Heaven was singing praises to God.

It just poured out of every leaf, rock, blade of grass, and every bird. It was the most beautiful sound I have ever heard. I can still hear it, even now, after all these years. It is like a song in the wind. Every now and then, I still hear the

Heavenly music, as the breeze blows through the leaves on the trees. It carries me back there and I feel that deep, all encompassing love again. It heals my soul and my spirit soars. There is no time in Heaven, so I have no idea how long it took for each different step of this journey.[13]

I was content to observe and enjoy this beautiful countryside: a countryside that emanated love from every side. The communication I had during the journey wasn't verbal, but I felt flooded with love, so that I didn't say anything. I enjoyed, and was delighted with this beautiful spectacle. I would have decided to stay here if I had had the choice. But I was like a balloon that leaves the hand of a child, and is not concerned with that which it leaves behind. It goes wherever the air takes it.[14]

I found myself in a city and was told that this was the City of God. This city had many different places all geared to a different need. There was a place of rest where souls could recover from traumatic lives on Earth. There were working places where souls could help mankind and others grow and be more.

There were libraries, theaters, and schools. And there was also the Temple of God. / I was shown a library filled with gold covered books. These are the lives of people on Earth where their life plan is laid out, and what they hope to achieve through certain key experiences.

I was shown other parts of the city as well where souls were working with people on Earth; scientists, the arts, and more. There is always a push there to 'inspire' those on Earth to create beneficial things for mankind in every area. This city had many different places all geared to a different need.

There was a place of rest where souls could recover from traumatic lives on Earth. There were working places where souls could help mankind and others grow and be more. There were libraries, theaters, and schools. And there was also the Temple of God. There was so much more too. But, more than anything this place was filled with love; love of mankind, love of everyone on Earth, and of the Earth itself. Communications were transparent there; thoughts shared as in a conversation here.

The people I saw were all working, happily so, and in great joy. Q It was more a sense of complete security and safety and difficult to describe visually. The buildings in the city looked like milk glass to some degree with veins of gold going through it. But there seemed to be a great deal of flexibility to its construction as well. Seats seemed to be able to mold to your shape.[15]

Then I saw a light very far away. I was surrounded by this unearthly loving, very beautifully radiating light. In that over-whelming radiating, loving light, I met a glowingly beautiful, very loving being. It was as if I knew him (it was apparently a he). I knew then that I knew him and felt completely comfortable and happy. His loving presence completely surrounded me and together we went through my life and all that I had experienced in a loving way, not any judging way.[16]

––––

I opened my eyes, and found myself in a cinema, with thousands of screens around me. Playing on every screen were episodes of the different moments in my 30 years of life, from early childhood till the present. Some of which I remembered, some of which I had long forgotten. I was intrigued by this fascinating experience, which I had never gone through or imagined. For the first time I had a simultaneous, panoramic picture of my entire life.[17]

––––

It was observed, and all the feelings involved during the life were examined. All was and felt good to see with him. While we were observing something particularly good, my good friend, this light being, made a kind of joyous outbreak of light and loving messages about what good I had done in that moment we had just observed.

We communicated with the use of our thoughts and mind. There were a lot of smiles and happiness related with the review of my life, even though my life was anything but easy. It had been tough, with many tears, betrayal, loneliness, abuse and more, but much joy with my grandparents and good playmates during my childhood, and later with my own children.

I could see it with him; endure it all without feeling a

single negative emotion through it, which is strange to think about afterwards. While there, in my Near-Death Experience, almost nothing made me wonder or question anything throughout the entire experience. Only much after, when I thought back, did I wonder about some of these experiences I had then.

I was told what was especially good, that also included experiences where I had acted with my heart, and not giving it any particular thought, this was really pointed out. In this way, I got to know what is especially good; to be and act with love and with the heart. To be happy and to be as good and pure in heart as possible with others.[18]

I saw where I had fallen short was mainly by omission. Sometimes by laziness or not wanting to complicate my life, I had not helped someone that needed it. At that moment, my hands were available for God to respond to a person in need.

I have tried hard to correct this, trying to see the best in others acting as a bridge for God to tell someone their worth, how beautiful they look, or how much they are loved by God and how important their friendship is. These may seem small and silly things but they are very important to some people at certain times.[19]

I soon found myself in a space and place unknown to me, having arrived there at a velocity I was unfamiliar with, with a force of attraction like that of metal to a magnet.[20]

When I arrived where I could not go forward... this is when I heard God's voice who talked to me, HIS VOICE stopped me. His voice has an ACTING energy power. While He was talking to me, I did feel I could not move anymore, although I very much wanted to reach the light.

My consciousness was clear, acute, this is a hyper-consciousness, ultra clear. Everything that has been told to me has been perceived and understood as being the TRUTH. This consciousness ENCOMPASSES ALL, just all. This is INSTANT consciousness. It is also different in the sense that communication is also realized through telepathy.

His presence (God's) was not a visual one, although I could have precisely said where He was, somewhat hidden in the shadow. His presence could be perceived through the energy mass I felt flowing out of Him and the place He was. He was God, no need to introduce Himself.

Not only does he communicate orally but also through telepathy, by placing TRUTHS in our mind. The fact that He was God was one of these truths he placed in my spirit. As for what has been expressed or transmitted; This was (when He talked to me) the most intense moment of my experience (God could read my thoughts); it is thus then that I had the highest level of consciousness and alertness.

God's voice was very clear; I could therefore clearly

identify the source. His voice was low and deep, as if it filled all, even myself inside. At the same time, His voice was quiet, pondered and acute, but full of authority and love. I say authority because at the time when I wanted to speak, I felt that HIS VOICE PREVENTED me from doing so: He read in my mind and answered the questions I had in my head.[21]

You are taught on the 'other side' what you are 'supposed to do,' but can you LIVE it under these pressures on Earth?...The other side does not have the physical pressures that having a body has. Here on Earth, you must feed and clothe that body and provide shelter for it from the elements. You are under continual pressure of some sort to make decisions that have a spiritual base....

From what I saw and heard there, on the other side, it is all about relationships and taking care of each other. Perfection is not expected of people but learning is expected and considered good progress. All of our experiences in a lifetime tend to follow some sort of pattern and often will recreate the same lessons only in a different way and under various circumstances. This is how you know what you are here to learn and test. If you examine the patterns, certain themes will become clear. I was shown a library filled with gold covered books.

These are the lives of people on Earth where their life plan is laid out, and what they hope to achieve through certain key experiences. From what I was shown, people have free choice as to how to get to these preset key experiences. They can take a meandering path of experiences or a more direct route, but there are certain events that are preset and will happen no matter what. Each of those key events are benchmarks and one's reactions to them will show how much you have learned and what more needs to be done, or learned.[22]

Then, I heard the voice of God in my head, and all at once, he asked me, 'Have you loved enough? Have you learned enough? Have you experienced enough?' I suddenly realized that I had not done the things he had asked of me, and I screamed, 'No!' I need to do more time.[23]

I was given the choice to leave life on earth and continue on, or, he recommended I return to earth and complete this life cycle. He said it was important to complete each life and its teachings before going on.[24]

I had one desire and one desire alone, to come back to this life and have this experience of rebirth while in a physical body. So he touched me on the forehead, smiling that compassionate smile, a smile of unlimited love deeper than any ocean you can think of, knowing we'll meet again and probably - again, sending me back to my physical body,[25]

Along with an overwhelming desire to return, I experienced guilt for not having thought of my wife and family during the NDE. They never even crossed my mind at the time. No desire to return to this life existed. Thoughts of suicide crossed my mind, not because I was unhappy in life, but because I was so content in death.

I later decided that life was like Disney World. I don't want to stay forever, but I'm not leaving until they throw me out of the park. What it is, I can't say. But there is most definitely something we experience after death. And it's wonderful. A sense that I was returning to this realm leads me to believe I have always existed, and will continue.[26]

The sensation was as if the most intense feeling of joy I had ever experienced had been amplified infinitely and was now a tangible thing that I was immersed in. It was so intense that the worry of the pain I knew my loved ones would feel over my departure was completely stripped away.

I understood that mortal life was such a temporary and brief experience. That all the pain I had ever experienced seemed so innocuous and benign, it was as if it had not ever mattered at all. The love and warmth felt so natural. I felt as if I had always felt this way and it had been taken away from me while I was alive.

It was if I had returned to the familiar after a long journey and was finally home at long last. Truly back home in that I knew deeply that I originated from there. I belonged there and my time on Earth suddenly felt so foreign and brief. My physical life felt like it was so long ago. I felt as if I was being showed what awaited me.

I knew that it was only available to me if I was worthy and that the circumstances of my passing did not warrant it. I knew then what mattered most in my life. The love I shared, the compassion I had for others, the kindness I displayed to everyone and ultimately how much of myself I gave to those I crossed paths with in my prior life.[27]

I realized that where I was, there was no religion and on no occasion were there people isolated or preaching one way as better, or worse than the rest. I believe that the mind of everyone is heaven or hell, they are not places. It is a state of consciousness that makes you be in one or the other place.

They never made me feel that just one religion had the truth. Absolutely! There is only one truth and that is within you, in your heart, and it is called love. Love doesn't confuse you, doesn't have limits or rules or errors: whereas religions do. I am not sure of what religion really provides for spiritual beings.

I believe they are a guide to help others but at least those of the western world, are better seen as manipulations of human beings to make them just the way they want to control them. I believe that the inner nourishment is the responsibility of each one of us, not of the church, as the church can have errors. I believe more in discovering methods to find inner peace and well-being in myself.[28]

I have to finish that which I promised even if I do not remember what it is. I have tried to give the best of me this time. Not to say that I have achieved it, but I will keep trying to be better each day of my life. I try to see things and people in a positive light. To enjoy and give thanks to God for each moment that I live, for the air that I breathe, the fruit, the flowers, the animals and my four children and grandchildren.

I wait impatiently (since it has been thirty-two years) for the day that I return home and rest from my passage through this life. I am not afraid of death, although I take good care of myself in order to keep my earthly vehicle in good condition and return it used but in working order.

I like life in this place, although I have suffered a lot. But is seems like this is the way that we learn and grow. I am not afraid of God; I feel only deep reverence toward him. I know that he is my loving father who is waiting for me and will welcome me with Love and Peace. The truth is that I want it to be over already - I want to return.

Thank God, my children are older now and will be able to continue with their life plans without me. Later we will see each other again. I have learned to see beyond appearances. I see in people their struggle to be better even though they do not always succeed. I have been called naive, silly, sometimes a hypocrite, because I get close to people that treat me badly and try to be their friend.[29]

The experience has left me with this feeling of being in limbo. Like, 'Why me?' I realize that we are without age. We have existed from the beginning, and we are without end. We are immortal. Nothing dies, it just transforms. We are perfection in the eye of the Creator.[30]

I hope you experienced as much joy reading *The Crossover Experience* as I did in writing it. Please leave an honest review by visiting our review page with the QR code below, or the review page of the retailer you purchased the book from. Know that reviews are an extremely helpful way for readers to discover independent authors. And I consider each and every review important feedback for my work.

About the Author

DJ Kadagian is an award-winning documentary film-maker, best-selling author, and quantum economist. His films have aired on PBS, Gaia TV, the Discovery Channel and Hallmark, as well as being featured at over 120 film festi-vals around the world. In his works he has collaborated with some of the country's top philosophers, academics, activists, poets, researchers and theologians. His thought-provoking works have focused on socioeconomic issues, race relations, religion & spirituality, and alternative healing.

DJ is also a hedge fund manager whose focus is within the discipline of technical analysis and quantum economics. He develops and manages proprietary, non-linear, quant-based investments strategies focused on the domestic commodity and equities markets. He is a Graduate of Cornell University and is a member of The Directors Guild of America. His latest book, *Punching Waves / A Memoir of Sorts* will be released in 2022. To learn more, visit www.4spStudio.com.

Pim van Lommel, M.D., born in 1943, graduated in 1971 at the University of Utrecht, and finished his specialization in cardiology in 1976. He worked from 1977-2003 as a cardiologist in Hospital Rijnstate, a 800 beds Teaching Hospital in Arnhem, the Netherlands, and is now doing full-time research on the mind-brain relation. He published several articles on cardiology, but since he started his research on near-death experiences (NDE) in survivors of cardiac arrest in 1986 he is the author of over 20 articles (most of them in Dutch), one book and many chapters about NDE. He was co-founder of the Dutch IANDS in 1988.

In 2005 he was granted with the Dr. Bruce Greyson Research Award of the International Association of Near-Death Studies (IANDS). In 2006, the president of India rewarded him the Life Time Achievement Award at the World Congress on Clinical and Preventive Cardiology in New Dehli. His Dutch book 'Endless Consciousness' was nominated for the 'Book of the Year 2008' in the Netherlands. In 2010 he received the 2010 Book Award van de Scientific and Medical Network, and in 2017 he received the Elisabeth Kübler-Ross Award by the Dutch Society of Volunteers in Palliative and Terminal Care (VPTZ). In 2020 the Spiritual Awakenings International (SAI) honored him for his ground-breaking work about Near-Death Experiences as Circle of Honor honoree.

In November 2007 his book 'Endless Consciousness' (Eindeloos Bewustzijn) was published in The Netherlands, now with more than 150.000 copies sold (26th edition). His book was published in Germany in 2009, and it was published in 2011 in the English language, entitled: Consciousness beyond Life. The science of the near-death Experience. It was also published in Polish, Spanish, French, Latvian, Italian, Hungarian and in Chinese. It will also be published in Russia. Over 300.000 copies have been sold worldwide. Visit his website at www.PimvanLommel.nl/en/

Gregory Shushan, PhD, is the leading authority on near-death experiences and the afterlife across cultures and throughout history. He is an Honorary Research Fellow at the Religious Experience Research Centre, University of Wales Trinity Saint David, and was previously Perrott-Warrick Researcher at University of Oxford's Ian Ramsey Centre for Science and Religion; and Scholar-in Residence at the Centro Incontri Umani (The Cross Cultural Centre), Ascona, Switzerland. He has lectured at universities in the UK, Ireland, and Switzerland and has given numerous talks on his research in nine countries.

He holds degrees in Religious Studies (University of Wales Lampeter), Research Methods for the Humanities, Egyptian Archaeology (University College London), and Eastern Mediterranean Archaeology (Birbeck College, University of London).

His work has been generously supported by grants from the Perrott-Warrick Fund at Trinity College Cambridge, the Arts and Humanities Research Council, the International Association for Near-Death Studies, the Cedar Creek Institute, the Alex Tanous Foundation for Scientific Research, and the Society for Psychical Research. For more information, visit his website at www.Gregory-Shushan.com

Come visit us!

To learn more about the phenomenon of the near-death experience, please visit us at the Crossover Experience website. There, you will find a treasure-trove of resources including a carefully curated collection of powerful NDE testimonials, interviews and lectures. You will also have access to the most important, peer-reviewed NDE research in downloadable format, as well as links to books and websites dedicated to the furthering of our understanding of the near-death experience.

www.CrossoverExperience.com

We hope to see you there!

Notes

1. INTRODUCTION

1. Pew Research Center, Nov. 3, 2015, "U.S. Public Becoming Less Religious"
2. Long J. (2014). Near-death experience. Evidence for their reality. *Missouri medicine*, *111*(5), 372–380.

2. What is a Near-Death Experience?

1. Noyes R Jr. Attitude change following near-death experiences. Psychiatry. 1980;43(3):234-42. doi: 10.1080/00332747.1980.11024070. PMID: 7403383.
2. Long J. (2014). Near-death experience. Evidence for their reality. *Missouri medicine*, *111*(5), 372–380.
3. Crossover Experience Retrospective Compilation:
   Peter Fenwick and Elizabeth Fenwick, The Truth in the Light (White Crow Books, 2012)
   Jeffrey Long and Paul Perry, Evidence of the Afterlife: The Science of the Near-Death Experience (New York: HarperCollins, 2009), 2-16.
   Greyson B. The near-death experience scale. Construction, reliability, and validity. J Nerv Ment Dis. 1983 Jun;171(6):369-75. doi: 10.1097/00005053-198306000-00007. PMID: 6854303.

4. A CROSSOVER EXPERIENCE I

1. "Michael H NDE," NDERF.org, https://www.nderf.org/Experiences/1michael_h_nde.html
2. "Benny M NDE," NDERF.org, https://www.nderf.org/Experiences/1benny_m_nde.html
3. "Randall J NDE," NDERF.org, https://www.nderf.org/Experiences/1randall_j_probable_nde.html
4. "Augustin NDE," NDERF.org, https://www.nderf.org/Experiences/1augustin_nde.html

5. "Tamara J NDE," NDERF.org, https://www.nderf.org/Experiences/1tamara_j_nde.html

6. "Nancy S NDE," NDERF.org, https://www.nderf.org/Experiences/1nancy_s_nde.html

7. "Pastor Dirk W," NDERF.org, https://www.nderf.org/Experiences/1dirk_w_nde.html

8. "Jeffrey B NDE," NDERF.org, https://www.nderf.org/Experiences/1jeffrey_b_nde.html

9. "Nancy S NDE," NDERF.org, https://www.nderf.org/Experiences/1nancy_s_nde.html

10. "Anthony M NDE," NDERF.org, https://www.nderf.org/Experiences/1anthony_m_nde_8596.html

11. "Monika NDE," NDERF.org, https://www.nderf.org/Experiences/1monika_nde.html

12. "Dan T NDE," NDERF.org, https://www.nderf.org/Experiences/1dan_t_nde.html

13. "Nancy S NDE," NDERF.org, https://www.nderf.org/Experiences/1nancy_s_nde.html

14. "Pastor Dirk W NDE," NDERF.org, https://www.nderf.org/Experiences/1dirk_w_nde.html

15. "Charlene P NDE," NDERF.org, https://www.nderf.org/Experiences/1charlene_p_nde.html

16. "Gillian M NDE," NDERF.org, https://www.nderf.org/Experiences/1gillian_m_nde.html

17. "Dr. Mary Neal", Youtube lecture transcript, published Nov 19, 2018, https://www.youtube.com/watch?v=OgGMTqR8Wt8&list=WL&index=3&ab_channel=St.John%27sCathedral

18. "Derry NDE," NDERF.org, https://www.nderf.org/Experiences/1derry_nde.html

19. "Tammie W NDE," NERF.org, https://www.nderf.org/Experiences/1tammie_w_nde.html

20. "John F NDE," NDERF.org, https://www.nderf.org/Experiences/1john_f_nde.html

21. "Thomas A ICU," NDERF.org, https://www.nderf.org/Experiences/1thomas_a_icu.html

22. "Bolette L NDE," NDERF.org, https://www.nderf.org/Experiences/1bolette_l_nde.html

23. "Benny M NDE," NDERF.org, https://www.nderf.org/Experiences/1benny_m_nde.html

24. "Jack NDE," NDERF.org, https://www.nderf.org/Experiences/1jack_nde.html

25. "Cynthia Y NDE," NDERF.org, https://www.nderf.org/ Experiences/1cynthia_y_nde.html
26. "Terry E NDE," NDERF.org, https://www.nderf.org/ Experiences/1terry_e_nde.html
27. "Gail A NDE ," NDERF.org, https://www.nderf.org/ Experiences/1gail_a_nde.html
28. "Tommy T NDE," NDERF.org, https://www.nderf.org/ Experiences/1tomy_t_nde.html
29. "Kelly K NDE," NDERF.org, https://www.nderf.org/ Experiences/1kelly_k_nde.html
30. "Gillian M NDE," NDERF.org, https://www.nderf.org/ Experiences/1gillian_m_nde.html
31. "Kelly K NDE," NDERF.org, https://www.nderf.org/ Experiences/1kelly_k_nde.html
32. "Augustin NDE," NDERF.org, https://www.nderf.org/ Experiences/1augustin_nde.html
33. "Shara G NDE," NDERF.org, https://www.nderf.org/ Experiences/1shara_g_nde.html
34. "Richard H NDE," NDERF.org, https://www.nderf.org/ Experiences/1richard_h_nde_3730.html
35. "Shara G NDE," NDERF.org, https://www.nderf.org/ Experiences/1shara_g_nde.html
36. "Lauren J NDE," NDERF.org, https://www.nderf.org/ Experiences/1lauren_j_nde.html
37. "Bolette L NDE," NDERF.org, https://www.nderf.org/ Experiences/1bolette_l_nde.html

6. Hard Statistics and Nuanced Observations

1. van Lommel P, van Wees R, Meyers V, Elfferich I. Near-death experience in survivors of cardiac arrest: a prospective study in the Netherlands. Lancet. 2001 Dec 15;358(9298):2039-45. doi: 10.1016/S0140-6736(01)07100-8. Erratum in: Lancet 2002 Apr 6;359(9313):1254. PMID: 11755611.
2. Parnia S, Waller DG, Yeates R, Fenwick P. A qualitative and quantitative study of the incidence, features and aetiology of near death experiences in cardiac arrest survivors. Resuscitation. 2001 Feb;48(2):149-56. doi: 10.1016/s0300-9572(00)00328-2. PMID: 11426476.
3. Schwaninger, Janet & Eisenberg, Paul & Schechtman, Kenneth & Weiss, Alan. (2002). A Prospective Analysis of Near-Death Experi-

ences in Cardiac Arrest Patients. Journal of Near-Death Studies. 20. 215-232. 10.1023/A:1015258818660.

4. Greyson, Bruce. (2003). Incidence and correlates of near-death experiences in a cardiac care unit. General hospital psychiatry. 25. 269-76. 10.1016/S0163-8343(03)00042-2.

5. Peter Fenwick and Elizabeth Fenwick, The Truth in the Light (White Crow Books, 2012)

6. Greyson B. The near-death experience scale. Construction, reliability, and validity. J Nerv Ment Dis. 1983 Jun;171(6):369-75. doi: 10.1097/00005053-198306000-00007. PMID: 6854303.

7. Schwaninger, Janet & Eisenberg, Paul & Schechtman, Kenneth & Weiss, Alan. (2002). A Prospective Analysis of Near-Death Experiences in Cardiac Arrest Patients. Journal of Near-Death Studies. 20. 215-232. 10.1023/A:1015258818660.

7. The Out-of-Body Experience

1. "Esteban FR NDE," NDERF.org, https://www.nderf.org/Experiences/1esteban_fr_nde.html

2. "Lael NDE," NDERF.org, https://www.nderf.org/Experiences/1lael_nde.html

3. "Halil T NDE," NDERF.org, https://www.nderf.org/Experiences/1halil_t_nde.html

4. "Karen M NDE," NDERF.org, https://www.nderf.org/Experiences/1karen_m_nde_8141.html

5. "Michael H NDE," NDERF.org, https://www.nderf.org/Experiences/1michael_h_nde.html

6. Dr. Mary Neal - NDE, NDE Stories, https://ndestories.org/dr-mary-neal/

7. "Nancy S NDE," NDERF.org, https://www.nderf.org/Experiences/1nancy_s_nde.html

8. "Tamara J NDE," NDERF.org, https://www.nderf.org/Experiences/1tamara_j_nde.html

9. "Shara G NDE," NDERF.org, https://www.nderf.org/Experiences/1shara_g_nde.html

10. "MVC NDE," NDERF.org, https://www.nderf.org/Experiences/1mvc_nde.html

11. "Michael H NDE," NDERF.org, https://www.nderf.org/Experiences/1michael_h_nde.html

12. "Rachel B NDE," NDERF.org, https://www.nderf.org/Experiences/1rachel_b_nde.html

13. "Christopher NDE," NDERF.org, https://www.nderf.org/ Experiences/1christopher_nde_6514.html
14. "Katie W NDE," NDERF.org, https://www.nderf.org/ Experiences/1katie_w_nde.html
15. "Ana Cecilia G NDE," NDERF.org, https://www.nderf.org/ Experiences/1ana_cecilia_g_nde.html
16. "Dr. Bell C NDE," NDERF.org, https://www.nderf.org/ Experiences/1bell_c_nde.html
17. "Destiny C NDE," NDERF.org, https://www.nderf.org/ Experiences/1destiny_c_nde.html
18. Crossover Experience Retrospective Compilation:
    Peter Fenwick and Elizabeth Fenwick, The Truth in the Light (White Crow Books, 2012)
    Jeffrey Long and Paul Perry, Evidence of the Afterlife: The Science of the Near-Death Experience (New York: HarperCollins, 2009), 2-16.
    Greyson B. The near-death experience scale. Construction, reliability, and validity. J Nerv Ment Dis. 1983 Jun;171(6):369-75. doi: 10.1097/00005053-198306000-00007. PMID: 6854303.
19. "About the Continuity of Consciousness – van Lommel, 2018 – The Galileo Commission." *The Galileo Commission*, 19 Mar. 2019, https:// galileocommission.org/about-the-continuity-of-consciousness-van-lommel-2018/.
20. Lommel, Pim. *Consciousness Beyond Life*. Harper Collins, 2011, p. 18.
21. Ibid.

8. The Tunnel Experience

1. "Shara G NDE," NDERF.org, https://www.nderf.org/ Experiences/1shara_g_nde.html
2. "John F NDE," NDERF.org, https://www.nderf.org/ Experiences/1john_f_nde.html
3. "Jaime G NDE," NDERF.org, https://www.nderf.org/ Experiences/1jaime_g_nde.html
4. "Craig P NDE," NDERF.org, https://www.nderf.org/ Experiences/1craig_p_nde.html
5. "Yvonne W NDE," NDERF.org, https://www.nderf.org/ Experiences/1yvonne_w_nde.html
6. "Irene L NDE," NDERF.org, https://www.nderf.org/ Experiences/1irene_l_nde.html
7. "Jeffrey B NDE," NDERF.org, https://www.nderf.org/ Experiences/1jeffrey_b_nde.html

8. "Benny M NDE," NDERF.org, https://www.nderf.org/Experiences/1benny_m_nde.html

9. "Charlie D NDE," NDERF.org, https://www.nderf.org/Experiences/1charlie_d_nde_4510.html

10. "Kelly K NDE," NDERF.org, https://www.nderf.org/Experiences/1kelly_k_nde.html

11. "Christine R NDE," NDERF.org, https://www.nderf.org/Experiences/1christine_r_nde.html

12. "John F NDE," NDERF.org, https://www.nderf.org/Experiences/1john_f_nde.html

13. "Benny M NDE," NDERF.org, https://www.nderf.org/Experiences/1benny_m_nde.html

14. "Tish Z NDE," NDERF.org, https://www.nderf.org/Experiences/1tish_z_nde.html

15. "Rene Hope Turner NDE," NDERF.org, https://www.nderf.org/Experiences/1rene_hope_turner_nde.html

16. "Anthony M NDE," NDERF.org, https://www.nderf.org/Experiences/1anthony_m_nde_8596.html

17. "Marisol HF NDE," NDERF.org, https://www.nderf.org/Experiences/1marisol_hf_nde.html

18. "Catherine D NDE, NDERF.org, https://www.nderf.org/Experiences/1catherine_d_nde.html

19. "Larisa NDE," NDERF.org, https://www.nderf.org/Experiences/1larisa_nde.html

20. "Mabel G Probable NDE," NDERF.org, https://www.nderf.org/Experiences/1mabel_g_probable_nde.html

21. "Halil T NDE," NDERF.org, https://www.nderf.org/Experiences/1halil_t_nde.html

22. "Laetitia V NDE," NDERF.org, https://www.nderf.org/Experiences/1laetitia_v_nde.html

23. "Dave G NDE," NDERF.org, https://www.nderf.org/Experiences/1dave_g_nde.html

24. Crossover Experience Retrospective Compilation:
    Peter Fenwick and Elizabeth Fenwick, The Truth in the Light (White Crow Books, 2012)
    Jeffrey Long and Paul Perry, Evidence of the Afterlife: The Science of the Near-Death Experience (New York: HarperCollins, 2009), 2-16.
    Greyson B. The near-death experience scale. Construction, reliability, and validity. J Nerv Ment Dis. 1983 Jun;171(6):369-75. doi: 10.1097/00005053-198306000-00007. PMID: 6854303.

25. Lommel, Pim. Consciousness Beyond Life. Harper Collins, 2011, p. 27.

9. Into the Light(s)

1. "Maria R NDE," NDERF.org, https://www.nderf.org/Experiences/1maria_r_nde.html
2. "Eben Alexander: A Neurosurgeon's Journey through the Afterlife," Youtube lecture transcript, published August 27, 2014, https://www.youtube.com/watch?v=qbkgj5J91hE&t=283s
3. "Jaime G NDE," NDERF.org, https://www.nderf.org/Experiences/1jaime_g_nde.html
4. "Joan D NDE," NDERF.org, https://www.nderf.org/Experiences/1joan_d_nde.html
5. "Giselle RV NDE," NDERF.org, https://www.nderf.org/Experiences/1giselle_rv_nde.html
6. "Sharon M NDE," NDERF.org, https://www.nderf.org/Experiences/1sharon_m_nde_7925.html
7. "Pastor Dirk W NDE," NDERF.org, https://www.nderf.org/Experiences/1dirk_w_nde.html
8. "Lloyd P NDE," NDERF.org, https://www.nderf.org/Experiences/1lloyd_p_nde.html
9. "B Rene A NDE," NDERF.org, https://www.nderf.org/Experiences/1jb_rene_a_nde.html
10. "Lael NDE," NDERF.org, https://www.nderf.org/Experiences/1lael_nde.html
11. "Andrew P NDE," NDERF.org, https://www.nderf.org/Experiences/1andrew_p_nde.html
12. "Catherine D NDE," NDERF.org, https://www.nderf.org/Experiences/1catherine_d_nde.html
13. "Linda B NDE," NDERF.org, https://www.nderf.org/Experiences/1linda_b_nde_4132.html
14. "Samson J NDE," NDERF.org, https://www.nderf.org/Experiences/1samson_j_nde.html
15. "Ana Cecilia G NDE," NDERF.org, https://www.nderf.org/Experiences/1ana_cecilia_g_nde.html
16. "Alice U NDE," NDERF.org, https://www.nderf.org/Experiences/1alice_u_nde.html
17. "Lauren J NDE," NDERF.org, https://www.nderf.org/Experiences/1lauren_j_nde.html
18. "Lauren J NDE," NDERF.org, https://www.nderf.org/Experiences/1lauren_j_nde.html
19. "Dr. Bell C NDE," NDERF.org, https://www.nderf.org/Experiences/1bell_c_nde.html
20. "Augustin NDE," NDERF.org, https://www.nderf.org/

Experiences/1augustin_nde.html
21. "Kerry B NDEs," NDERF.org, https://www.nderf.org/ Experiences/1kerry_b_ndes.html
22. Crossover Experience Retrospective Compilation:
    Peter Fenwick and Elizabeth Fenwick, The Truth in the Light (White Crow Books, 2012)
    Jeffrey Long and Paul Perry, Evidence of the Afterlife: The Science of the Near-Death Experience (New York: HarperCollins, 2009), 2-16.
    Greyson B. The near-death experience scale. Construction, reliability, and validity. J Nerv Ment Dis. 1983 Jun;171(6):369-75. doi: 10.1097/00005053-198306000-00007. PMID: 6854303.

10. Deceased Loved Ones & Spiritual Beings

1. "Jesse N NDE," NDERF.org, https://www.nderf.org/ Experiences/1jesse_n_nde.html
2. "Anthony M NDE," NDERF.org, https://www.nderf.org/ Experiences/1anthony_m_nde_8596.html
3. "Rene Hope Turner NDE," NDERF, https://www.nderf.org/ Experiences/1rene_hope_turner_nde.html
4. "John F NDE," NDERF.org, https://www.nderf.org/ Experiences/1john_f_nde.html
5. "Douglas T NDE," NDERF.org, https://www.nderf.org/ Experiences/1douglas_t_nde.html
6. "Halil T NDE," NDERF.org, https://www.nderf.org/ Experiences/1halil_t_nde.html
7. "Destiny C NDE," NDERF.org, https://www.nderf.org/ Experiences/1destiny_c_nde.html
8. "Alice U NDE," NDERF.org, https://www.nderf.org/ Experiences/1alice_u_nde.html
9. "Anne NDE," NDERF.org, https://www.nderf.org/ Experiences/1anne_nde.html
10. Mary Neal Describes Her Visit to the Gates of Heaven, Mark Galli | December 6, 2012 Interview
    https://www.christianitytoday.com/ct/2012/december-web-only/ mary-neal-describes-her-visit-to-gates-of-heaven.html
11. "Jaime G NDE," NDERF.org, https://www.nderf.org/ Experiences/1jaime_g_nde.html
12. "Eben Alexander: A Neurosurgeon's Journey through the Afterlife," Youtube lecture transcript, published August 27, 2014, https://www. youtube.com/watch?v=qbkgj5J91hE&t=283s

13. "Archie M NDE ," NDERF.org, https://www.nderf.org/Experiences/1archie_m_nde.html

14. "David NDE," NDERF.org, https://www.nderf.org/Experiences/1david_nde_6562.html

15. "Glenn F NDE," NDERF.org, https://www.nderf.org/Experiences/1glenn_f_nde.html

16. Mary Neal Describes Her Visit to the Gates of Heaven, Mark Galli | December 6, 2012 Interview
https://www.christianitytoday.com/ct/2012/december-web-only/mary-neal-describes-her-visit-to-gates-of-heaven.html

17. Crossover Experience Retrospective Compilation:
Peter Fenwick and Elizabeth Fenwick, The Truth in the Light (White Crow Books, 2012)
Jeffrey Long and Paul Perry, Evidence of the Afterlife: The Science of the Near-Death Experience (New York: HarperCollins, 2009), 2-16.
Greyson B. The near-death experience scale. Construction, reliability, and validity. J Nerv Ment Dis. 1983 Jun;171(6):369-75. doi: 10.1097/00005053-198306000-00007. PMID: 6854303.

18. Lommel, Pim. *Consciousness Beyond Life*. Harper Collins, 2011, p. 32.

11. The NDE Environment

1. "Lauren J NDE," NDERF.org, https://www.nderf.org/Experiences/1lauren_j_nde.html

2. "Zenaida NDE," NDERF.org, https://www.nderf.org/Experiences/1zenaida_nde.html

3. "Halil T NDE," NDERF.org, https://www.nderf.org/Experiences/1halil_t_nde.html

4. "Bill W NDE," NDERF.org, https://www.nderf.org/Experiences/1bill_w_nde.html

5. "Tommy T NDE," NDERF.org, https://www.nderf.org/Experiences/1tomy_t_nde.html

6. "Pastor Dirk W NDE," NDERF.org, https://www.nderf.org/Experiences/1dirk_w_nde.html

7. "Anne NDE," NDERF.org, https://www.nderf.org/Experiences/1anne_nde.html

8. Jung, C. G. *Memories, Dreams, Reflections*. Vintage, 2011.

9. "Sharon M NDE ," NDERF.org, https://www.nderf.org/Experiences/1sharon_m_nde_7925.html

10. "Jerry B NDE," NDERF.org, https://www.nderf.org/Experiences/1jerry_b_nde.html

11. "Julian D NDE," NDERF.org, https://www.nderf.org/Experiences/1julian_d_nde.html

12. "Scott Drummond - Pronounced Dead for 20 Minutes - What He Saw and How it Changed His Life Forever," Youtube interview transcript, published May 27, 2020, https://www.youtube.com/watch?v=a8jcNBVWJyE&ab_channel=PrioritizeYourLife

13. "Dr. Rick U NDE," NDERF.org, https://www.nderf.org/Experiences/1rick_u_nde.html

14. "Saundra V NDE," NDERF.org, https://www.nderf.org/Experiences/1saundra_v_nde.html

15. "491 Anne NDE," NDERF.org, https://www.nderf.org/Experiences/1anne_nde.html

16. "Taylor NDE," NDERF.org, https://www.nderf.org/Experiences/1taylor_nde.html

17. "Don C NDE," NDERF.org, https://www.nderf.org/Experiences/1don_c_nde.html

18. "Jack M NDE," NDERF.org, https://www.nderf.org/Experiences/1jack_m_nde_6168.html

19. "Sharon M NDE," NDERF.org, https://www.nderf.org/Experiences/1sharon_m_nde_7925.html

20. "Cynthia Y NDE," NDERF.org, https://www.nderf.org/Experiences/1cynthia_y_nde.html

21. Crossover Experience Retrospective Compilation:

    Peter Fenwick and Elizabeth Fenwick, The Truth in the Light (White Crow Books, 2012)

    Jeffrey Long and Paul Perry, Evidence of the Afterlife: The Science of the Near-Death Experience (New York: HarperCollins, 2009), 2-16.

    Greyson B. The near-death experience scale. Construction, reliability, and validity. J Nerv Ment Dis. 1983 Jun;171(6):369-75. doi: 10.1097/00005053-198306000-00007. PMID: 6854303.

12. The Five (+) Senses

1. "Bolette L NDE," NDERF.org, https://www.nderf.org/Experiences/1bolette_l_nde.html

2. "Dan T NDE," NDERF.org, https://www.nderf.org/Experiences/1dan_t_nde.html

3. "Shara G NDE," NDERF.org, https://www.nderf.org/Experiences/1shara_g_nde.html

4. "Andrew P NDE," NDERF.org, https://www.nderf.org/Experiences/1andrew_p_nde.html

5. "Charles T NDE," NDERF.org, https://www.nderf.org/Experiences/1charles_t_nde_8594.html

6. "Dr. Bell C," NDERF.org, https://www.nderf.org/Experiences/1bell_c_nde.html

7. "Kelly K NDE," NDERF.org, https://www.nderf.org/Experiences/1kelly_k_nde.html

8. "Mr. W NDE," NDERF,org, https://www.nderf.org/Experiences/1mr_w_nde.html

9. "Jack M NDE," NDERF.org, https://www.nderf.org/Experiences/1jack_m_nde_6168.html

10. "Roger M NDE," NDERF.org, https://www.nderf.org/Experiences/1roger_m_nde.html

11. "Murry M NDE," NDERF.org, https://www.nderf.org/Experiences/1murry_m_nde.html

12. "Jesse N NDE," NDERF.org, https://www.nderf.org/Experiences/1jesse_n_nde.html

13. "Lauren J NDE," NDERF.org, https://www.nderf.org/Experiences/1lauren_j_nde.html

14. "Monika NDE," NDERF.org, https://docs.google.com/spreadsheets/d/1SQcMMzsWLKnApoxUx7SyzNTdht9kYYgxoV6Gvat69Dw/edit#gid=67537645

15. "Sharon M NDE," NDERF.org, https://www.nderf.org/Experiences/1sharon_m_nde_7925.html

16. "David NDE," NDERF.org, https://www.nderf.org/Experiences/1david_nde_6562.html

17. "Mr. W NDE," NDERF.org, https://www.nderf.org/Experiences/1mr_w_nde.html

18. "Ana Cecilia G NDE," NDERF.org, https://www.nderf.org/Experiences/1ana_cecilia_g_nde.html

19. "Dr. Mary C. Neal Recalls Her Inspiring Near-Death Experience | Guideposts." *Guideposts*, 7 Nov. 2017, https://www.guideposts.org/inspiration/life-after-death/dr-mary-c-neal-recalls-her-inspiring-near-death-experience.

20. Crossover Experience Retrospective Compilation:

    Peter Fenwick and Elizabeth Fenwick, The Truth in the Light (White Crow Books, 2012)

    Jeffrey Long and Paul Perry, Evidence of the Afterlife: The Science of the Near-Death Experience (New York: HarperCollins, 2009), 2-16.

    Greyson B. The near-death experience scale. Construction, reliability, and validity. J Nerv Ment Dis. 1983 Jun;171(6):369-75. doi: 10.1097/00005053-198306000-00007. PMID: 6854303.

13. The Life Review

1. "Dannion Bringley," NDEstories.org, https://ndestories.org/dannion-brinkley/
2. "Mike M NDE," NDERF.org, https://www.nderf.org/Experiences/1mike_m_nde.html
3. "Dr. Bell C NDE," NDERF.org, https://www.nderf.org/Experiences/1bell_c_nde.html
4. "Mike M NDE," NDERF.org, https://docs.google.com/spreadsheets/d/1SQcMMzsWLKnApoxUx7SyzNTdht9kYYgxoV6Gvat69Dw/edit#gid=1113578778
5. Williams, Kevin. (2002). Nothing Better Than Death; Insights From Sixty-Two Profound Near-Death Experiences.
6. "John F NDE," NDERF.org, https://www.nderf.org/Experiences/1john_f_nde.html
7. "Bolette L NDE," NDERF.org, https://www.nderf.org/Experiences/1bolette_l_nde.html
8. "Glenda H NDE," NDERF.org, https://www.nderf.org/Experiences/1glenda_h_nde_3045.html
9. "Katie W NDE," NDERF.org, https://www.nderf.org/Experiences/1katie_w_nde.html
10. "Marten M NDE," NDERF.org, https://www.nderf.org/Experiences/1marten_m_nde.html
11. "Andrew P NDE," NDERF.org, https://www.nderf.org/Experiences/1andrew_p_nde.html
12. "Giselle RV NDE," NDERF.org, https://www.nderf.org/Experiences/1giselle_rv_nde.html
13. "Jean R NDE," NDERF.org, https://www.nderf.org/Experiences/1jean_r_nde_6166.html
14. "Chapter 5 - Near-Death Experiencer Reinee Pasarow - The Greatest Of All Actions," Youtube lecture transcript, published May 11, 2017, https://www.youtube.com/watch?v=R7J0BZHRFoE
15. Crossover Experience Retrospective Compilation:

    Peter Fenwick and Elizabeth Fenwick, The Truth in the Light (White Crow Books, 2012)

    Jeffrey Long and Paul Perry, Evidence of the Afterlife: The Science of the Near-Death Experience (New York: HarperCollins, 2009), 2-16.

    Greyson B. The near-death experience scale. Construction, reliability, and validity. J Nerv Ment Dis. 1983 Jun;171(6):369-75. doi: 10.1097/00005053-198306000-00007. PMID: 6854303.

14. In the Presence of God

1. "Terry E NDE," NDERF.org, https://www.nderf.org/Experiences/1terry_e_nde.html
2. "Mark H NDE," NDERF.org, https://www.nderf.org/Experiences/1mark_h_nde.html
3. "Mabel G Probable NDE," NDERF.org, https://www.nderf.org/Experiences/1mabel_g_probable_nde.html
4. "Hera A NDE," NDERF.org, https://www.nderf.org/Experiences/1hera_a_nde.html
5. "Kerry B NDE," NDERF.org, https://www.nderf.org/Experiences/1kerry_b_ndes.html
6. "JB Rene A NDE," NDERF.org, https://www.nderf.org/Experiences/1jb_rene_a_nde.html
7. "Shannon C NDE," NDERF.org, https://www.nderf.org/Experiences/1shannon_c_nde.html
8. "Sharon M NDE," NDERF.org,https://www.nderf.org/Experiences/1sharon_m_nde_7925.html
9. "Nathan L NDE," NDERF.org, https://www.nderf.org/Experiences/1nathan_l_nde.html
10. "Erica P NDE," NDERF.org, https://www.nderf.org/Experiences/1erica_p_nde.html
11. "Andy B NDE," NDERF.org, https://www.nderf.org/Experiences/1andy_b_nde.html
12. "Kerry B NDE," NDERF.org, https://www.nderf.org/Experiences/1kerry_b_ndes.html
13. "Chris M NDE," NDERF.org, https://www.nderf.org/Experiences/1chris_m_nde.html
14. "Roger M NDE," NDERF.org, https://www.nderf.org/Experiences/1roger_m_nde.html
15. "Katie W NDE," NDERF.org, https://www.nderf.org/Experiences/1katie_w_nde.html
16. "Raven R NDE," NDERF.org, https://www.nderf.org/Experiences/1raven_r_nde.html

15. The Knowledge of Everything

1. "Benny G NDE," NDERF.org, https://www.nderf.org/Experiences/1benny_g_nde.html

2. "Yazmine S NDE," NDERF.org, https://www.nderf.org/Experiences/1yazmine_s_nde.html

3. "Charles T NDE," NDERF.org, https://www.nderf.org/Experiences/1charles_t_nde_8594.html

4. "William R NDE," NDERF.org, https://www.nderf.org/Experiences/1william_r_nde.html

5. "Tamara J NDE," NDERF.org, https://www.nderf.org/Experiences/1tamara_j_nde.html

6. "Romona B NDE," NDERF.org, https://www.nderf.org/Experiences/1romona_b_nde.html

7. "Sharon M NDE," NDERF.org, https://www.nderf.org/Experiences/1sharon_m_nde_7925.html

8. "Kelly K NDE," NDERF.org, https://www.nderf.org/Experiences/1kelly_k_nde.html

9. "William C NDE," NDERF.org, https://www.nderf.org/Experiences/1william_c_nde.html

10. "Andrew P NDE," NDERF.org, https://www.nderf.org/Experiences/1andrew_p_nde.html

11. "Romona B NDE," NDERF.org, https://www.nderf.org/Experiences/1romona_b_nde.html

12. "Shara G NDE," NDERF.org, https://www.nderf.org/Experiences/1shara_g_nde.html

13. "Annie V NDE ," NDERF.org, https://www.nderf.org/Experiences/1annie_v_nde.html

14. "Jean R NDE," NDERF.org, https://www.nderf.org/Experiences/1jean_r_nde_6166.html

15. "Jack M NDE," NDERF.org, https://www.nderf.org/Experiences/1jack_m_nde_6168.html

16. "Lauren J NDE," NDERF.org, https://www.nderf.org/Experiences/1lauren_j_nde.html

17. "Thomas M NDE," NDERF.org, https://www.nderf.org/Experiences/1thomas_m_nde_3958.html

18. "Jean R NDE," NDERF.org, https://www.nderf.org/Experiences/1jean_r_nde_6166.html

19. "Jeanne MK NDE," NDERF.org, https://www.nderf.org/Experiences/1jeanne_mk_nde.html

20. Crossover Experience Retrospective Compilation:

    Peter Fenwick and Elizabeth Fenwick, The Truth in the Light (White Crow Books, 2012)

    Jeffrey Long and Paul Perry, Evidence of the Afterlife: The Science of the Near-Death Experience (New York: HarperCollins, 2009), 2-16.

    Greyson B. The near-death experience scale. Construction, reliability, and validity. J Nerv Ment Dis. 1983 Jun;171(6):369-75. doi: 10.1097/00005053-198306000-00007. PMID: 6854303.

21. *"Pim Van Lommel Consciousness and The Near Death Experience" Interview by Iain McNay.* YouTube, 23 May 2013, https://www.youtube.com/ watch?v=glKccJ5YUcg.

22. *Ibid.*

23. *Ibid.*

24. *Ibid.*

16. It is Not Your Time

1. "Lauren J NDE," NDERF.org, https://www.nderf.org/ Experiences/1lauren_j_nde.html

2. "Irene L NDE," NDERF.org, https://www.nderf.org/ Experiences/1irene_l_nde.html

3. "Jack NDE," NDERF.org, https://www.nderf.org/ Experiences/1jack_nde.html

4. "Tommy T NDE," NDERF.org, https://www.nderf.org/ Experiences/1tomy_t_nde.html

5. "Flora S NDE," NDERF.org, https://www.nderf.org/ Experiences/1flora_s_nde.html

6. "Augustin NDE," NDERF.org, https://www.nderf.org/ Experiences/1augustin_nde.html

7. "Benny M NDE," NDERF.org, https://www.nderf.org/ Experiences/1benny_m_nde.html

8. "Tamara J NDE," NDERF.org, https://www.nderf.org/ Experiences/1tamara_j_nde.html

9. "Jesse N NDE," NDERF.org, https://www.nderf.org/ Experiences/1jesse_n_nde.html

10. "Deborah S NDE," NDERF.org, https://www.nderf.org/ Experiences/1deborah_s_nde.html

11. "Ana Cecilia G NDE,", NDERF.org, https://www.nderf.org/ Experiences/1ana_cecilia_g_nde.html

12. "Kelly K NDE," NDERF.org, https://www.nderf.org/ Experiences/1kelly_k_nde.html

13. "Shara G NDE," NDERF.org, https://www.nderf.org/ Experiences/1shara_g_nde.html

14. "Charles T NDE," NDERF.org, https://www.nderf.org/Experiences/ 1charles_t_nde_8594.html

15. "Earl M NDE," NDERF.org, https://www.nderf.org/ Experiences/1earl_m_nde.html

16. "Anna   BZ   NDE   ,"   NDERF.org,   https://www.nderf.org/Experiences/1anna_bz_nde.html
17. "Don   C   NDE,"   NDERF.org,   https://www.nderf.org/Experiences/1don_c_nde.html
18. "Giselle   RV   NDE,"   NDERF.org,   https://www.nderf.org/Experiences/1giselle_rv_nde.html
19. Crossover Experience Retrospective Compilation:
     Peter Fenwick and Elizabeth Fenwick, The Truth in the Light (White Crow Books, 2012)
     Jeffrey Long and Paul Perry, Evidence of the Afterlife: The Science of the Near-Death Experience (New York: HarperCollins, 2009), 2-16.
     Greyson B. The near-death experience scale. Construction, reliability, and validity. J Nerv Ment Dis. 1983 Jun;171(6):369-75. doi: 10.1097/00005053-198306000-00007. PMID: 6854303.
20. Lommel, Pim. *Consciousness Beyond Life*. Harper Collins, 2011, p. 40-41.
21. *"Pim Van Lommel Consciousness and The Near Death Experience" Interview by Iain McNay*. YouTube, 23 May 2013, https://www.youtube.com/watch?v=glKccJ5YUcg.

17. The Hellish Realm

1. "Patricia C NDE," NDERF.org, https://www.nderf.org/Experiences/1patricia_c_nde_6841.html
2. "Jaime   G   NDE   ,"   NDERF.org,   https://www.nderf.org/Experiences/1jaime_g_nde.html
3. "James   S   NDE,"   NDERF.org,   https://www.nderf.org/Experiences/1james_s_nde.html
4. "Dian S Probable NDE," NDERF.org, https://www.nderf.org/Experiences/1dian_s_probable_nde.html
5. "Jedraine   C   NDE,"   NDERF.org,   https://www.nderf.org/Experiences/1jedraine_c_nde.html
6. "Charles   T   NDE,"   NDERF.org,   https://www.nderf.org/Experiences/1charles_t_nde.html
7. "Thomas   A   ICU,"   NDERF.org,   https://www.nderf.org/Experiences/1thomas_a_icu.html
8. "Marina   A   NDE,"   NDERF.org,   https://www.nderf.org/Experiences/1marina_a_nde.html
9. "Tammie   W   NDE,"   NDERF.org,   https://www.nderf.org/Experiences/1tammie_w_nde.html
10. "MVC   NDE,"   NDERF.org,   https://www.nderf.org/Experiences/1mvc_nde.html

11. "Jean R NDE," NDERF.org, https://www.nderf.org/Experiences/ ljean_r_nde_6166.html
12. "Dr. Rajiv Parti – DNDE, NDE," NDEstories.org, https://ndestories. org/dr-rajiv-parti/
13. Crossover Experience Retrospective Compilation:
    Peter Fenwick and Elizabeth Fenwick, The Truth in the Light (White Crow Books, 2012)
    Jeffrey Long and Paul Perry, Evidence of the Afterlife: The Science of the Near-Death Experience (New York: HarperCollins, 2009), 2-16.
    Greyson B. The near-death experience scale. Construction, reliability, and validity. J Nerv Ment Dis. 1983 Jun;171(6):369-75. doi: 10.1097/00005053-198306000-00007. PMID: 6854303.

18. Religion on the Other Side

1. "Jean R NDE," NDERF.org, https://www.nderf.org/Experiences/ ljean_r_nde_6166.html
2. "Thomas A ICU," NDERF.org, https://www.nderf.org/ Experiences/1thomas_a_icu.html
3. "Tamara J NDE," NDERF.org, https://www.nderf.org/ Experiences/1tamara_j_nde.html
4. "Zachary G NDE," NDERF.org, https://www.nderf.org/ Experiences/1zachary_g_nde.html
5. "Giselle RV NDE," NDERF.org, https://www.nderf.org/ Experiences/1giselle_rv_nde.html
6. "Dan P NDE," NDERF.org, https://www.nderf.org/ Experiences/1dan_p_nde.html
7. "Karen M NDE," NDERF.org, https://www.nderf.org/Experiences/ 1karen_m_nde_8141.html
8. "Kerry B NDEs," NDERF.org, https://docs.google.com/ spreadsheets/d/ 1SQcMMzsWLKnApoxUx7SyzNTdht9kYYgxoV6Gvat69Dw/ edit#gid=598727742
9. "Dr. Mary Neal – NDE," NDEstories.org, https://ndestories.org/dr- mary-neal/
10. "Rachael C NDE," NDERF.org, https://www.nderf.org/ Experiences/1rachael_c_nde.html
11. "Teresa C NDE," NDERF.org, https://www.nderf.org/ Experiences/1teresa_c_nde.html
12. "Mr. W NDE," NDERF.org, https://www.nderf.org/ Experiences/1mr_w_nde.html

13. "Arvind   B   NDE,"   NDERF.org,   https://www.nderf.org/Experiences/1arvind_b_nde.html
14. "Jedraine   C   NDE,"   NDERF.org,   https://www.nderf.org/Experiences/1jedraine_c_nde.html
15. "Jean R NDE," NDERF.org, https://www.nderf.org/Experiences/1jean_r_nde_6166.html
16. "Julian   D   NDE,"   NDERF.org,   https://www.nderf.org/Experiences/1julian_d_nde.html
17. Lommel, Pim. *Consciousness Beyond Life*. Harper Collins, 2011, p. 56.
18. Ibid., 58.

19. How NDEs Change Everyone

1. "Lloyd   P   NDE,"   NDERF.org,   https://www.nderf.org/Experiences/1lloyd_p_nde.html
2. "Dr. Rick U NDE," NDERF.org, https://www.nderf.org/Experiences/1rick_u_nde.html
3. "Anthony   M   NDE,"   NDERF.org,   https://www.nderf.org/Experiences/1anthony_m_nde.html
4. "Kerry   B   NDEs,"   NDERF.org,   https://www.nderf.org/Experiences/1kerry_b_ndes.html
5. "Linda B NDE," NDERF.org, https://www.nderf.org/Experiences/1linda_b_nde_4132.html
6. "Mr.   W   NDE,"   NDERF.org,   https://www.nderf.org/Experiences/1mr_w_nde.html
7. "Tammie   W   NDE,"   NDERF.org,   https://www.nderf.org/Experiences/1tammie_w_nde.html
8. "Charlene   P   NDE,"   NDERF.org,   https://www.nderf.org/Experiences/1charlene_p_nde.html
9. "Romona   B   NDE,"   NDERF.org,   https://www.nderf.org/Experiences/1romona_b_nde.html
10. "Mike   M   NDE,"   NDERF.org,   https://www.nderf.org/Experiences/1mike_m_nde.html
11. "Charlene   P   NDE,"   NDERF.org,   https://www.nderf.org/Experiences/1charlene_p_nde.html
12. "Linda B NDE," NDERF.org, https://www.nderf.org/Experiences/1linda_b_nde_4132.html
13. "Romona   B   NDE,"   NDERF.org,   https://www.nderf.org/Experiences/1romona_b_nde.html
14. "Chris   M   NDE,"   NDERF.org,   https://www.nderf.org/Experiences/1chris_m_nde.html

15. "Tanya NDE," NDERF.org, https://www.nderf.org/ Experiences/1tanya_nde.html
16. "Karen M NDE," NDERF.org, https://www.nderf.org/Experiences/ 1karen_m_nde_8141.html
17. "Lloyd P NDE," NDERF.org, https://www.nderf.org/ Experiences/1lloyd_p_nde.html
18. "Ana Cecilia G NDE," NDERF.org, https://www.nderf.org/ Experiences/1ana_cecilia_g_nde.html
19. "Esteban FR NDE," NDERF.org, https://www.nderf.org/ Experiences/1esteban_fr_nde.html
20. "Tish Z NDE," NDERF.org, https://www.nderf.org/ Experiences/1tish_z_nde.html
21. "Elaine J NDE," NDERF.org, https://www.nderf.org/ Experiences/1elaine_j_nde.html
22. "Tamara J NDE," NDERF.org, https://www.nderf.org/ Experiences/1tamara_j_nde.html
23. "Bolette L NDE," NDERF.org, https://www.nderf.org/ Experiences/1bolette_l_nde.html
24. Long J. (2014). Near-death experience. Evidence for their reality. *Missouri medicine*, *111*(5), 372–380.
25. Russell Noyes Jr. (1980) Attitude Change Following Near-Death Experiences, Psychiatry, 43:3, 234-242, DOI: 10.1080/00332747.1980.11024070
26. "About the Continuity of Consciousness – van Lommel, 2018 – The Galileo Commission." *The Galileo Commission*, 19 Mar. 2019, https:// galileocommission.org/about-the-continuity-of-consciousness-van-lommel-2018/.

20. A CROSSOVER EXPERIENCE II

1. "Thomas M NDE," NDERF.org, https://www.nderf.org/ Experiences/1thomas_m_nde_3958.html
2. "Taylor NDE," NDERF.org, https://www.nderf.org/ Experiences/1taylor_nde.html
3. "Benny M NDE," NDERF.org, https://www.nderf.org/ Experiences/1benny_m_nde.html
4. "Taylor NDE ," NDERF.org, https://www.nderf.org/ Experiences/1taylor_nde.html
5. "Giselle RV NDE," NDERF.org, https://www.nderf.org/ Experiences/1giselle_rv_nde.html

6. "Thomas M NDE," NDERF.org, https://www.nderf.org/Experiences/1thomas_m_nde_3958.html

7. "Ana Cecilia G NDE," NDERF.org, https://www.nderf.org/Experiences/1ana_cecilia_g_nde.html

8. "Roger E NDE," NDERF.org, https://www.nderf.org/Experiences/1roger_e_nde.html

9. "Mr. W NDE," NDERF.org, https://www.nderf.org/Experiences/1mr_w_nde.html

10. "Wendy G NDE," NDERF.org, https://www.nderf.org/Experiences/1wendy_g_nde.html

11. "Earl M NDE," NDERF.org, https://www.nderf.org/Experiences/1earl_m_nde.html

12. "Wendy G NDE," NDERF.org, https://www.nderf.org/Experiences/1wendy_g_nde.html

13. "Sharon M NDE," NDERF.org, https://www.nderf.org/Experiences/1sharon_m_nde_7925.html

14. "Ana Cecilia G NDE," NDERF.org, https://www.nderf.org/Experiences/1ana_cecilia_g_nde.html

15. "Jean R NDE, NDERF.org, https://www.nderf.org/Experiences/1jean_r_nde_6166.html

16. "Bolette L NDE," NDERF.org, https://www.nderf.org/Experiences/1bolette_l_nde.html

17. "Dr. Bell C NDE," NDERF.org, https://www.nderf.org/Experiences/1bell_c_nde.html

18. "Bolette L NDE," NDERF.org, https://www.nderf.org/Experiences/1bolette_l_nde.html

19. "Giselle RV NDE," NDERF.org, https://www.nderf.org/Experiences/1giselle_rv_nde.html

20. "Augustin NDE," NDERF.org, https://www.nderf.org/Experiences/1augustin_nde.html

21. "Catherine D NDE," NDERF.org, https://www.nderf.org/Experiences/1catherine_d_nde.html

22. "Jean R NDE," NDERF.org, https://www.nderf.org/Experiences/1jean_r_nde_6166.html

23. "Christine R NDE," NDERF.org, https://www.nderf.org/Experiences/1christine_r_nde.html

24. "William R NDE," NDERF.org, https://www.nderf.org/Experiences/1william_r_nde.html

25. "Jesse N NDE," NDERF.org, https://www.nderf.org/Experiences/1jesse_n_nde.html

26. "Jack M NDE," NDERF.org, https://www.nderf.org/Experiences/1jack_m_nde_6168.html

27. "Mr. W NDE," NDERF.org, https://www.nderf.org/Experiences/1mr_w_nde.html

28. "Ana Cecilia G NDE," NDERF.org, https://www.nderf.org/Experiences/1ana_cecilia_g_nde.html

29. "Giselle RV NDE," NDERF.org, https://www.nderf.org/Experiences/1giselle_rv_nde.html

30. "Tish Z NDE," NDERF.org, https://www.nderf.org/Experiences/1tish_z_nde.html

Acknowledgments

The authors gratefully acknowledge the support and encouragement of the following authors, publishers, and researchers:

Quoted testimonials from the Jody and Jeffery Long, M.D., Near Death Experience Research Foundation (NDERF), www.NDERF.org

Quotes from *Consciousness Beyond Life*, by Pim van Lommel, MD. Copyright 2010 by Pim van Lommel. Reprinted by permission of HarperCollins Publishers.

Lightning Source UK Ltd.
Milton Keynes UK
UKHW011817210822
407560UK00004B/111/J